#LAZARUS10

#LAZARUS10

Book One
The Lake Pen Series

Andrew Rajan

San Fernando Press

ISBN 978-0-9930687-3-7
First Edition published 2016
by

San Fernando Press

ISBN 978-0-9930687-3-7

Typeset by ebookscoversdesign.com

About the author

Andrew Rajan started out as a Mechanical Engineer, training as an apprentice at the Ministry of Defence. Having globe-trotted, he studied at the Guildhall School, thereafter appearing in various British TV, such as EastEnders, Casualty, Soldier, Soldier and The Bill as well as BAFTA award-winning dramas Loved Up and Holding On and Hollywood's The League of Extraordinary Gentlemen. Tiring of the stereotyped roles he was offered, he moved over to storytelling.

As a filmmaker, he produced Fox/Lottery-funded Short Losing Heart, then made rom-com feature Offending Angels, as director, producer, creating lead roles for non-white actors eschewing colour and culture as the reason for their story, premiering at Raindance Film Festival, 2002.

Thereafter, he gained an MA with Commendation at the National Film & Television School, where he made controversial sexual politics Short 'Opportunist', later picked up by FoxTV. Two privately commissioned feature-length documentaries followed and then feature film, 'Greys Inbetween'.

Andrew has served the BAFTA jury, the Sony Radio Awards and the RTA Television Awards, amongst others. He has written three stage plays - 'Mental', 'Afghanistan' and 'That Paki Play'.

Three novels 'Cathedrals In The Sky', 'The Big Game' and '#Lazarus10'.

He has also written five feature screenplays.

Find out more and subscribe at www.andrewrajan.com

Acknowledgements

Debs, Georgie, Vic, Roy, Marco and Sean, my thanks to you all for your part in the creation.

I'd also like to thank Hilary at Kruger Media for all her input, work and expertise.

For Kit

1

You'll know me by now. Everybody does. Antonio Pesic, also known as Tony Peso. The guy going down for killing people already dead. The guy who offered the impossible ride: The last ten seconds of life. Over and over, if you could afford it. That, robbing banks of billions and taking down the FBI. That is to say, everyone thinks they know me, know my story, but the one that's become the legend, as is so often the case, isn't half of what happened.

Even today, I know very little about cryogenics, or more accurately cryonics and, when all this first kicked off, I knew even less. What I did know though, was an opportunity when I saw one. When it all started I was living in a little studio flat with a garden, a poorly converted Victorian terrace, the neighbours from Hell living above me, my overgrown garden home to a young fox I'd taken to calling Memphis, who seemed to have a weird fetish for used nappies. I'd find them strewn across my ivy-leaf lawn, all bloated with rain or morning dew. Wrapping my hand in a shopping bag I'd go out, holding my breath as I gingerly tied it off to deposit in the bin, knowing it a futile gesture, as there'd surely be another come tomorrow. You might guess, I never had kids.

Cryogenics, for those of you who picked this book up by mistake, is the study of materials at exceedingly low temperatures. 'Cryonics' is the application of this branch of science to preserving human remains once they've died, in the hope that, as science evolves, they might be brought back to life at some point in the future. The breakthroughs being made in the past decade being as rapid and stupendous as they are, even I, in my ignorant day-to-day life had been made aware that the process of preservation had been markedly improved from those early days towards the end of last century. Still, you had to be pretty well off to give it a go; well, middle-class anyway.

It's surprising how much money is out there. Once you get to the end and tot up your fiscal sum, taking into account property prices in the city, or the country spread you relaxed into, the nest egg, the portfolio, the second home or boat, the cars, the heirlooms, the artwork and few oddments of collectible furniture dotted about the place. Once cryonics proved itself to be much more of a real deal than anybody had really anticipated (through Yours Truly, I might add), down-in-the-mouth kids were looking forward to a drastically reduced inheritance, because mum and dad had latently decided to bury a good lump of their net worth into a personalised subterranean stainless steel fridge for the foreseeable. And why not? They'd earned it.

I made so many millionaires, in so many unforeseen

ways... they made more money than I ever saw- and still are to this day. It's a billion -soon to turn trillion- dollar industry. Like mobile phones. Cryonics labs sprang up not just across America, but the entire Western-Eastern-Southern world and by the thousands, by the tens of thousands. Germany, Britain, Scandinavia, France, Switzerland, Austria, Belgium, Australia -even as far as Tokyo, Beijing, Kuala Lumpur and Hong Kong. Singapore. Needless to say, it went bananas across the Middle East. Suddenly, everyone was an expert, everybody wanted in, either this side, earning the money, or the other for the pregnant promise of Life After Death.

I singlehandedly turned the stock market upside-down overnight: Made stainless steel casing manufacturers turn millionaire to billionaire. Bottled gas companies, piping companies, fixtures and fittings suppliers, temperature control electronics geeks, security providers, logistics, marketing, even previously unwanted property prices went through the roof in the mad scramble for suitable realty. The guys who really cashed in though were the cryonics companies who were there at the start, they were the ones with the head-start, the ones who could say 'we're the genuine article', the 'original and best', there at the beginning. They made an absolute killing. The whole thing went Totally Nuts. And I was sitting on it all, all on my own-some. I mean, don't get me wrong, I'm nobody's fool, I saw it was big, really big and we made a stinking huge pile of dough out of it, enough for several lifetimes, but even I didn't see how big.

How did it all start? It's hard to know where to begin really.. It wasn't a lightbulb moment I don't think, more an accumulation of things, a series of seemingly unconnected events, both circumstantial and mental that took me to that crossroads in Time, where Everything Changed. I do know for certain that if I had arrived at that exact same situation without the other stuff happening also, I probably wouldn't have made the same decisions, or even seen it for the opportunity it was.

2

The place I was at was a classic one, boring in its unoriginality. I would read about suicide statistics and knew I hit the bracket: Male, 30-44. What lead me to this? Under the veneer of North London mediocrity, I was at screaming pitch. I knew it, I just didn't know what to do about it... do with that energy. I saw men around me, head down, a wild look in their eye, drinking to quiet the voice, to manacle the impulse, but ready to jump at the throat of anyone who appeared confrontational. It wasn't an answer but then, what was? I saw a Chinese horoscope once which reckoned I had in me the seeds either of fame, or notoriety, but so far, those pips hadn't blossomed into anything recognisable, in either direction. They had however sewn a thread of deep disquiet, malcontentedness, of anger: A core frustration, that left me staring at the bedroom ceiling for hours at a time through the day, when I was meant to be sleeping.

Inert on the nightshift at work for hours at a time, I would read every day of men making a success of their lives, scanning the print for their age. If they were older, it relieved the pressure somewhat, but if younger, or even worse, the same age, I would feel a sense of panic rise in my gut, threatening to overwhelm me. Why them? Why not me? Why couldn't it happen to me? What had I done so wrong? Was it Fate? Did I believe in Fate?

On some level I knew that money didn't buy happiness, that fame was a double-edged sword, driving people to madness, to strange excess, going under the knife, or buying in to ridiculous symbols of success, marrying trophy wives, or finally being caught for serial indiscretions, their haunted visages plastered across every unsavoury magazine, every rag on the stand. And yet... and yet I still wanted wealth. I still ached for fame. I still needed to hit the EuroMillions jackpot at 93 million and be forced to work out how best to spend, who would benefit and where I might begin to invest the rest of it. As if I knew with ease what so many who had gone before didn't, in terms of what to do with such astronomical amounts of cash. And so it seemed, whenever I stopped to look, that I was just four paces away from a fork in the road, looking left and right. One way was more of the same. A tacit capitulation. A bowing of the head, a defocussing of the eyes, signifying that from here on I simply accepted my lot, allowed whatever dreams or aspirations I may have had as a younger man to die in the shadows, gagged, bound, uncelebrated, the bones crumbling into unmarked graves.

The other headed upward, into sunshine. It smelt of flowers and clean smiles. Of open-necked linen shirts and an arm around a slim-waisted beauty staring adoringly at my cheekbone, as I looked steadily into the gold-tipped future. I just had no idea how to make those strides that would propel me forward onto that path. But I wasn't standing still, I was moving inexorably forward, but my will was on rails, rails heading past that sought after turning and I felt powerless to stop me. Powerless to change trajectory, even though I could see it and knew it was a genuine option.

Burying myself in an endless online search... I kidded myself it was for love, but I knew it was something far more insubstantial than that. A figment that didn't exist... and yet I persisted.

Almost exactly one year later, I was sealing the deal that would net me my first million. Yanks, they like a show. They like mystery. And people with money, they seek the unique and, as I learned, would pay anything to get it. Usually, these days that meant a one off experience, or item: An autographed Jimi Hendrix guitar. Usain Bolt's 100m winning running shoes (with one lace undone). That car from 'Back To The Future'. A private party with a top name guesting in the garden, a celebrity chef cooking ridiculously exclusive ingredients aboard the private jet, on the way to a meeting with the Dalai Lama.

Now, sitting here in my cell, a sharpening trapezoid of light travelling too quickly over impassive walls, across unforgiving floor, it was difficult to reconcile how different my life had become and how fast. I realised I was glad I didn't have a parent alive to witness it.

3

I'd been round to see my dad on my day off. He lived on his own in an upmarket, old school, one floor apartment in Highgate. He'd been there a while. It was one of those really peaceful, purpose-built places with heavy doors and ornate tiling in the hallway, a gardener tending the abundant foliage in the leafy approach to the generous gloss-black Victorian double doors.

I let myself in, calling out as I wiped my feet on the outsized doormat, the third I'd encountered on the way in. He was in his early 80's, but I couldn't remember whether he was 82 or 83. Maybe 84. Something like that. I'd come round to fit a few handles about the place, so he could get himself up easily. He walked with a sort of three-wheel stroller that enabled him to put whatever he was reading in a shallow basket infront of him and, taking mini quick-steps, he would shuffle noiselessly along the thick carpet.

He was a sweet man, never tall at his prime, he was positively petite now. I say he was a sweet man and he was, but his disappointment in me was palpable. A Luthier, he used to make violins and loved Shakespeare's sonnets... could recite any number of them off by heart, even when he couldn't remember whether the gas was left on, what day of the week it was. His disappointment in me was that I had my feet more firmly planted on the ground than he. I never tilted my face up to the stars, never aspired to anything 'great' or 'artistic'. Not even altruistic. He never said anything directly, but his bemusement was obvious; how could the product of a concert pianist mother and poet father amount to nothing more than a security guard? I wasn't creative in any shape or form. Nor did I take any interest in the arts, even as interested observer. He was a Romantic in the truest sense of the word. I knew it, I recognised it for what it was. I was no slouch, I had a good education that both my parents augmented after school and at weekends, but it became very obvious by my teenage years that I wasn't going to be practicing anything either of them might regard with relish or enthusiasm.

Do I care about this? I guess so, but then, if you aren't that thing, you aren't; there's no point in pretending. I could recognise talent when I saw it, but it didn't reside in me. Not that kind of talent anyway. I was quite practical though and this I did learn from my father, watching him bent over a slim shim of wood, coaxing it shaving it, loving it into shape over many hours. A lamplit workshop stuffed to the gunnels with any number of delicate, wood handled tools with names like chisel, gimlet and scratch awl. Sticky tins and bottles of varnish and stain, filler and oil, glue and grease. Aromatic, seasoned blocks of maple, ebony, spruce, willow, rose and boxwood. It was as magical, as fragrant as any imagined Egyptian perfumery. He'd spent his life creating, hands and mind.

The District Nurse had been around with some kind of Occupational Therapist, who had marched through his home making a list of what was required. I was tasked with putting up five short hand rails, two in the loo and three in the bathroom. There were some helpful pencil 'x's marked on the wall where they were needed, some positioned at a forty-five degree angle. The solid, ribbed plastic rails themselves, piled on the old trunk in the hall didn't come with screws but, Dad being Dad, he had a good stack to choose from. I used really long, thick ones, determined that the wall itself would come down before they came loose, diligently drilling and rawl-plugging the holes, pressing the screws firmly home with my DeWalt.

Just two days later he was gone. I wasn't with him when he died. His regular carer away on holiday, it was the Temp Help that found him, seemingly still fast asleep, she'd let herself in and had several minutes conversation with his corpse from the kitchen, actually made him a cup of milky tea and some toast before she realised he wasn't going to be getting up that morning.

I always figured if you made it to your eighties, it could be said that you'd had a good innings and he'd had a good innings: Married the love of his life- after a brief misstep with a Mile End seamstress- then moved to Finchley and had me. His was a fulfilled life, he'd never asked too much of it and had been very content making beautiful and well-received musical instruments. Looking around his workshop, there were no unfinished symphonies. He'd made the last one he was going to make with the very last of the wood he had and then, with a satisfied sigh, hung up his tools on the board for the last time, safe in the knowledge that he had done his level best and every string out there with his mark on it had been given all the care and attention that he was capable of giving. When he retired, it was as if he had completely used up every ounce of his allotted energy and expertise, that there wasn't another drop in him to give.

I stood in the doorway of the crematorium chapel, greeting family friends, relatives and his many acquaintances as they filed past and found a seat. As I eventually took my own place at the front, listening to a string quartet, followed by eulogies and poems, I reflected perhaps predictably on my own mortality, on the fleeting nature of a life that speeded up, the older you got.

Mum had died almost nine years previously, taking herself off to her motherland Switzerland to die and be buried there. When I thought of it, I suppose I had always believed that he would go first, small and frail as he was, so her passing was a shock to everyone. It was touch and go how he might cope with the loss; whether he might toss in the towel and stop eating, go into a spiral depression, like a cat whose owner has gone on holiday and, for a time, all he would focus on was the funeral and nothing beyond it. But once that was done, he did look forward, made enquiries how best to cook for one, as he'd never cooked in his life before that time. Never used a washing machine. But he changed gears, got himself off to recitals, took walks in nearby woods and sat in the garden watching the wind in the leaves, the squirrels and magpies. He took to listening to the radio, previously something that only mum had done. Perhaps as company, or as a reminder, who knows.

As I desperately wiped my eyes in order to actually see the curtain drop on him for the final time, I realised I needed to make changes. Big ones, if I was to look back as my father must have done, to smile at my achievements, at my memories.

Two things jolted me into action. The first was a piece read by my uncle, which he basically read at me from the lectern. It was meant as life advice, but the way he read it, it was clearly a message from Dad, principally for my ears. It comprised three things: If you don't pursue that which you want, you'll never have it. If you don't actually ask, the answer will always be no. If you don't step forward, you will remain in the same place.

I'd had versions of this same conversation with myself many a time, sitting at some faceless reception desk, offices closed for the night, one eye on the static image of the carpark on the monitor and the other on my screen, flicking through whatever took my fancy. I hadn't gone to school thinking afterwards I'd really fancy a job where I sat for days on end, wishing someone would break-in just to relieve the boredom, hour upon hour upon hour. I preferred the nightshift though. I preferred my own company. I didn't understand the guys who took jobs in department stores, standing all day in a silly uniform, frowning at anyone who stepped over the heat-blown threshold, challenging them to shoplift.

As with anything now, Security meant qualifications, meant training: You had to take a course that covered First Aid, basic defence moves, understanding fire extinguishers, their coding and operation, evacuation protocol, an understanding of some of the laws pertaining to body-searching and restraining people, but once the Home Office issued you with an SIA badge, you realised the difficult bit was actually landing a job. You needed to know someone, or you were stuffed.

Fortunately for me, I got on well with my instructor Arif, who seemed relieved I actually had something between the ears and could speak English with a modicum of ease. I realised how rare this was when I met the other guys attending the course with me. So in the days after the course ended we exchanged a few banter messages and then he called up with a gig, working the door at a club. I didn't want to do it, I'd heard enough horror stories of doormen getting stabbed or glassed by disgruntled drunk punters, male and female, but then figured if I took it, it might lead to better things, so I did.

The evening passed well enough, I was one of six, so managed to miss most of the really frontline stuff. I was hardly built to be a doorman anyway, so there was this unspoken agreement with the seasoned veterans that I would do the less demanding stuff and they would take care of the pointy end. It suited me. Thereafter, I was again called up, this time for a night gig covering for a guy who'd gone a bit doollally, as he'd been doing nightshifts on a building site seven days a week 9pm to 7am, for nine months solid. So I stepped in and liked it; I liked that I wasn't going to face vomiting girls, testosterone teenagers and loud, thumping music all night.

But I also knew my dad had a point. It wasn't a vocation. It wasn't testing me, trying me, offering any palpable reward beyond short-term money. I didn't want to do it forever, I just didn't know what I did want in its place. I wanted to travel, I wanted to fall in love or, failing that, get laid a lot with women I found attractive. And then fall in love. I wanted to meet famous and interesting people, but I had no real idea how to realise any of these things. It seemed to need a huge amount of cash and a social ease or standing that simply wasn't within my grasp, whichever way I turned it around in my mind. It was easy to see why people lost themselves in TV series or hobbies. From all the countless, indistinguishable days I'd already spent, one thing was clear; life would pass you by, whether you got involved or not.

The second thing that caused me finally to act was money. A rather sizeable lump sum, upon the resolution of my parents estate. That and going through my father's papers. I'd got through a fair amount before, but in the final clear out I came across a dusty deed box from his bank, containing a bunch of papers going back to his early years. It appeared he'd spent some time dealing in business, wheeling and dealing in stocks and shares, or some such. I didn't really need to follow the ins and outs, as I was already well aware of what he was worth. He'd never really seemed interested in money and the figures bore that out: He'd done ok, but he certainly hadn't set the financial world alight. Just well enough to set himself up handsomely, buy a nice house and start his instrument business in a small but well-appointed shop rented in Mayfair. He'd never mentioned that chapter that I could recall, but then, most people had more than one career in their pursuit of financial security. Interesting to find out that he had a bit of gamble in him though.

The first thing I did was pay off my flat. The one thing I had done as a security guard was make good inroads into my mortgage, so paying it off didn't swallow a huge amount and I had a pretty good chunk left over. But without the monthly payments to worry about, it was easy then to jack in the job, lounge about the flat and start thinking seriously about travel. I had mates in many corners of the world. Some of them not corners I particularly wished to see; Moscow, Nepal or Dubai, for instance, but others did appeal; Australia for example, Thailand, Tobago and the States- Los Angeles, Chicago, New York. Then there were places like New Zealand, Hawaii and Fiji that were just begging to be seen, regardless of the fact I knew no one there. The more I dwelt on it, there were places nearer home too, like Rome, Paris, Berlin, Copenhagen, Prague and Barcelona.

I definitely needed to sort out a trip. Or maybe a series of trips. Perhaps I should go on a few shorter ones to get a feel for it and then venture further afield. Or just say 'bugger it' and go off on a 'round the world and take two years to do it' sort of a jaunt. It felt entirely different from how it was before, when you just went off on holiday. The framework had completely changed. I wasn't going away for two weeks to Greece, the South of France, Majorca, or wherever. It felt like an opportunity not just to travel, but to find something out about myself. Who I was perhaps, or at least what it was I wanted to do for the rest of my life. Maybe I'd even meet someone.

4

All in all, I felt tired and a bit wired. I didn't have the energy or focus to arrange anything too epic, rent out the flat and everything, but used a recommended travel agent to sort me out a flexible ticket that went LA, Hawaii, Australia, New Zealand, Fiji, LA and home. So long as I used it in a year, I could adjust the time I stayed in any one place to suit myself. The first thing I needed to do was renew my passport, my old one not far off being out of date. I went for the fatter, more expensive one, confident that this year would be the start of something much more adventurous.

I got my neighbour Ruth to come in and check the place from time to time, go through any post, with instructions to throw everything away, unless it was important. I could tell she loved the idea of opening my mail, but I didn't mind particularly. I'd long since dispensed with bank statements and everything of import was on standing order. She wasn't up to speed with computers let alone emails, so I suggested in an emergency, that she leave me a message by phoning my landline, assuring her I'd be able to pick up any voicemail remotely.

Handing in my notice was easy, all I needed to do was get someone to cover and there was never a shortage of willing security guards. Whether they were any good was the issue, but it wasn't my concern. I made the call to my instructor friend Arif and he said he would get on it. He was always trying to get his guys work, the ones he liked anyway, so it was nice to do him a favour, albeit a small one.

"Arif."

"You in trouble? What kinda trouble you in?"

I'm not in trouble. I'm going away though. Dunno how long. A year maybe. Look, I need cover for my gig at GNTS. They're expecting me back but..."

"I can do that. Where you headed?"

"LA. For now."

"LA. That ain't so bad. I got my people out there. You need anything, let me know. I hook you. I hook you.. You want numbers? I get you numbers.. Hold on.." He said.

I always found myself getting a bit more street than I was when talking to people more street than me. I think it was purely in an effort to fit in. I just mimicked those around me. Got me into trouble sometimes though, them thinking I was taking the piss. I did try to resist.

"No it's ok Arif. I don't need.. I'm just going for a break, not long, you know, then heading up Hawaii. I won't be there, you know."

"Ok. Hawaii. Well, you need a break man. Hakuna matata."

"Hakuna matata? Is that.. Hawaii? I think that's Swahili..."

"Is it? I don't know do I? Swahili? It was in that film." He said.

"What film?"

"You know, all the animals and shit.. Old Cartoon.. Lion. Aaahh, you know.. It's right there.. Madagascar!"

"Yeah. That's Africa." I said.

"Oh yeah. Haha. Well have a great trip bro. You take care."

"Thanks bro. So.. You need the guy up and running to start Tuesday eve, right? You got their number. Course you do. You got me the gig." I said.

"Yeah, don't worry, I got your back. I gotta go, I'm on something here."

Arif had about three to six girls circling him at any given time. Obviously, he liked one or two of them more than the others, but it seemed a constant merry go round. The first time we met outside of training, I ended up giving him a bunch of advice. That is to say, I listened a lot and then tried to help him work out which girl he fancied the most. I tend to be able to talk a better game than I execute, put it that way.

Apart from Security, Arif was also a successful drug dealer and, when things had been tight, had even made money from extortion. With his crew working the doors at the all best nightclubs in London, he used to supply pills to clubbers, taking out any potential competition via body searches. It was perfect. I guess it paid to understand the criminal fraternity, if you were going to work in the trade.

I put my three pot plants on the low front wall, sure that someone would have them, if only for the pots and dumped the last of the fridge food in the wheelie bin. My phone rang again. It was Arif.

"LA? You're going to LA?"

"Yah. Right now."

"You're leaving right now?"

"Yeah. Why?"

"What airport?"

"Heathrow."

"What time's your flight? You driving? How you getting there?"

"No, I'm tubing it.."

"Who uses the tube, bro? Look. You tube it to mine and I give you a lift. Ok? I need you to do something.."

"Is it dodgy?" I already knew the answer.

"Course not. You come by me?"

"Ok. Sure."

As I Chubb-locked the front door, secreting the keys in my hand luggage, little did I know I'd never see the inside of my flat again.

On my way to the Edgware Road, I tried to conjecture what he might want. To carry something to LA was the best bet, but what, I couldn't work out. Papers? I knew I wasn't carrying drugs, for sure, but I also knew he wasn't that stupid.

I buzzed up when I got to his tower block, nodding as I did so to the bored security guard on the concierge desk. Arif came down almost immediately. I was impressed, it wasn't like him. Aside from his jacket, he held a package. We got to his Maserati, I put my suitcase in the back and slid into the red leather passenger seat. No need for air fresheners, the cockpit simply smelt expensive. It wasn't til we were smoothing down the A40 that he raised the subject.

"Can you do me a favour?"

I looked at him by way of response. We'd already done this bit.

"I need to get a package to my cousin."

"What is it?" I knew I wouldn't get any kind of a straight answer, but it was worth asking, if only to glean what I could from how he answered.

"Don't worry, it's only a drive. I told you.."

"A drive?"

"A hard drive."

My mind sped up with myriad possibilities.

"What's on it?"

He looked at me for the first time.

"Nothing you need to worry about. But I need to get it there, pronto."

I wondered for a moment whether there was even a drive in it and it wasn't just stuffed with smack, but it didn't make any sense that it would be. I smiled and looked out the window. The car was deceptively fast and we were doing an effortless 65 in a 30 limit. The real question was not so much 'was it dodgy', but more, 'was I prepared to take it, knowing it was'.

"What's in it for me?"

"What you thinking?"

"Well, what happens if I get stopped at the airport and they find it on me? What happens then?"

"Nothing, bro. Nothing at all. There's nothing there they can do you for."

I looked at him.

"Word of honour, bro. It's sound."

"No risk..?"

"No risk."

"So.. It's hard to put a price on it, right, if everything's as you say, right? But then, if it was safe to FedEx, you'd just FedEx, right? So I don't know what to say."

"Ok, so I give you, say.. A grand and I owe you. How's that?"

Again, he gave me something to ponder. A favour from Arif was a useful thing, certainly not something to be taken lightly. He was a guy plugged into many things, he knew a lot of people. I figured a grand was cheap.. I could ask for more; if he felt it was worth a grand, it was worth at least ten times that, it went without saying. But to push him up to five grand seemed a little pointless. I didn't really need the money, not at that level. But to have a marker, that had value, even if right now, I didn't know how I might spend it. It felt a good thing to have.

"It's just a drive." He repeated.

"Ok, bro. I'll do it."

He beamed a toothy smile, genuinely relieved and we bumped fists. Interesting. It was much bigger than he was letting on, but I also reflected that right now, with two lines of airport security to get through, it was probably just as well I didn't know anything more; less to get stressed about.

"I knew you wouldn't let me down."

He passed me an envelope with a phone number on it.

"Message me when you land. I'll have a guy meet you. He'll get you to my cuz and then he'll get you a cab wherever you want to go."

I nodded at the bag on the back seat.

"Is that it?"

He nodded and I reached around and opened the bag and the neoprene casing that couched it. It looked like a drive. I hefted it, sniffing the grill, hoping it might betray itself, but it looked and felt sound.

"What's his name? Your Cuz?"

"Sammie. He's like my brother. He'll look after you."

We slowed up inside the airport carpark complex, stopping at drop offs.

"Here." He passed me a solid wedge of currency. I looked at it.

"What's that?"

"A grand."

I grinned. I didn't need to count it. But it was in US Dollars.

"Wanker."

"You're going to LA, aren't you? Thought I'd do you a favour."

Getting out, I tucked the drive in my hand luggage. Turning to say goodbye, he clapped me on the shoulder.

"Thanks for the lift."

"Be good." The request had an edge to it, barely perceptible, but there, nonetheless. Towing my luggage, I turned to go. Loud enough to embarrass me, he then said -

"Use it to buy condoms. They'll love your accent."

I didn't break stride, not needing to turn around to hear him pull away, the massive engine angry at being held in check, still managed to announce its departure.

Once safely through security and fancying some champagne, I found an oyster bar.

Ok, so this was a turn up. All the great stories tell of someone recognising the calling when they are offered adventure and here I was, already up in proceedings with a wedge of dollars in my pocket. But I really couldn't work out for the life of me what could be on the drive that wouldn't just as easily have been sent over by DropBox, or whatever, if it wasn't currency. What could it possibly be?

Maybe it was just a test, a dry run for something more dangerous they were lining up in the future... for the trip home. Or maybe it was just some kind of practical joke he was playing either on his cousin, or at my expense. If they were even related.

Information. That's what was always on drives, ones and noughts. So it might be files, MI5, CIA, or something. Espionage. Stolen ID's.. Bank details. A lot of bank details on a drive this big. Any which way, I'd made a grand. I finished my glass and made my way to the Departure lounge. It hadn't tasted as sweet as I hoped.

It just didn't make sense and like some mental Rubik's Cube, I turned it over and over countless times above the Atlantic. I took a moment to pull out the dollars and discretely make sure they weren't fake, then looked out at the light blinking on the wingtip against distant clouds.

It was so easy to travel. You just got on a plane and a few hours later, stepped onto the tarmac of a completely different country. It was extraordinary when you stopped to think about it. I don't suppose many people did these days.

5

Tired of being single and not managing to pull at the rate and ferocity of my beefcake club-scene security co-workers, I'd been hitting the online dating scene quite hard and from several angles over the past few years. Starting out quite meekly with a standard profile on Match then, when that didn't work overly well, expanding upwards, as well as down. By that I mean I tried some more expensive, exclusive sites and also got drawn into the murkier side of instant hook ups and Russian Brides.

The real trouble with the instant hook up sites was what to put there. The only profiles I was really drawn to were ones where the women were brave (foolish?) enough to show their faces. Not all though. Some needed far less. It got me thinking however, that if I was to progress at all on there, I needed to do the same, but I really wasn't inclined at all. The obvious thing to do was a cock shot, but I wasn't comfortable with that either, so I left that bit blank and simply went exploring to see what I could see. It really was quite possible to lose oneself for the best part of an evening; five hours or more, a week to ten days just perusing photos. And once I'd been on there even a short amount of time as a freeloading perv, I had quite a number of cold offers, more than I'd experienced on the straight sites anyway, promising threesomes, mostly with husbands watching, even though all I'd done was put up a false age, hair colour and average height. It didn't appeal though.

Tinder was the most brutal. You swiped right if you liked someone and left if you didn't. The ultimate in throw away. Some younger girls, around 18 to 25 made no bones about what they were after. In one description she dispensed even with any emoticons, offering a only PayPal button with the words 'make a deposit'.

What it did get me thinking about was becoming a male escort. It's a male fantasy right, to get paid to get taken somewhere really swanky, then on to a hotel and obliged to have sex. I looked into it. One guy seemed to have got there first. He'd nailed and linked all the websites to one and seemed to have a really comprehensive knowledge and listing of how it was done, how to pay by card, what the rules were and even testimonies. It was all pretty intimidating and made me realise, as with most things, that if you really wanted to make a go of it, then you were going to need to spend a lot of time and energy making it happen. I couldn't set up some tinpot website with a rubbish holiday snapshot and expect the offers to come rolling in.

Upon further investigation there were organisations that specialised in being the middleman whereby, for a fee, you could advertise your wares on their site and then sit back and await the call. One drunk night, I decided this was the way forward and paid the thirty five quid fee, sending in a picture I felt did me justice. But thereafter, I looked at the huge number of men already selling themselves and realised I really didn't stand a cat's chance in Hell of getting selected. Besides, what if someone I knew saw me up on there? I'd die of shame.

The next thing I buried myself in for quite a while was so-called Russian dating. There were any number of sites and an absolute avalanche of beautiful women all seemingly holding their breath just waiting for me to arrive. After all, I wasn't some overweight sixty-year-old American, I was fit and young. All I had to do was invest in buying tokens, that were then spent messaging the girl of my choice. Some were more expensive to chat to than others, normally the more beautiful, the more in demand, the more they cost. At the same time I enrolled in a chat forum for men seeking love in the new USSR.

It was enlightening, not to say sobering. As I dug deeper and spent the time on the forum threads, it soon became apparent that most of the sites I had enrolled in were scams. I was more likely to be messaging a Yuri than a Yulia: Some fat geezer smoking toxic, knock-off cigarettes, who cut and pasted lovelorn messages of sweetness and the occasional additional pic to keep me buying.

There were some great stories there though from guys who had done it, done it the hard way and eventually bought up a ticket and gone out to meet them. It turned out there was a billion dollar business in taking men on 'tours' of Russia to meet women, to cough up for transport, for hotels, flowers, translators and parties, to learn Russian. Kerching.

Then there were the horror stories of guys who actually made it work, paid the necessary fees, went over time after time, set their girls up in apartments in some village three hours out of Vladivostok; got the paperwork done and finally brought them over to the US, only to find out it was a tissue of lies and all she was wanting was the Greencard and some hot young stud, once she obtained the dual nationality. It was a minefield. Whoever said love was easy?

Having spent a fair amount of money and ogling the long way round, I eventually located a couple of forums that discussed in depth the challenges apparent to the Western man hoping to date a Russian hottie and bring her home. It smashed through the scam sites, the ones set up purely as a money making exercise of which there are several, turning over millions of dollars. The men weighed in with the plusses and minuses of doing a tour, where you paid to take in several cities and either met women you were already in touch with online, or simply blind-dated several hundred at arranged parties. Every way you turned, you were the ATM.

The seasoned experts spoke of getting the girl fixed up with her own wifi, that you funded, so at least that way, you could have direct communication when and wherever you wanted it. It also indicated to the girl that you were serious about her and not just a sex tourist. They also advocated learning Russian, even though you were hoping to bring them over at some point in the future, in the belief that it lead to better relations, trust and understanding, at an earlier point.

It all looked a little difficult to achieve. And also expensive, without any guarantees either of finding someone, or that the whole enterprise wasn't a scam from start to finish. You didn't need to delve very deep to uncover the horror stories, where it had all gone wrong. The vast majority of these were American, because the vast majority of the forum contributors were Yanks. Most stories spoke of the difficulties and scams along the way, women melting into the ether, that existed as nothing more than a photo in the first place, but there were also harum-scarum stories of women who had gone through all the motions, declared love for their partner, got through the necessary US Border hurdles and then, once installed in the US of A, finally revealed their true colours. One had a Russian boyfriend and proceeded to bring not only him, but her whole family over on her ticket, installing them in the poor man's home. He was bullied into submission and didn't feel he could do anything about it, too aware he'd been a fool in the first place to think some hot-to-trot 26 year old model might be interested in a bald, 48-year-old electronics engineer from Iowa.

It made for sober reading. I reluctantly withdrew interest from the Russian conundrum; however appetising the images were, that's all they were after all, pictures. Besides, the cultural differences really were pronounced. Life experience counted for quite a lot more than I had previously realised.

At the same time, I was dragged sideways into the world of the dating gurus. Men with testosterone-driven monikers who'd evidently made millions of pounds selling their secrets and techniques for getting any woman they wanted into bed. There was a plethora of videos tackling various problems or skill-sets on offer, all available at a premium. There were also two-day seminars promising one-on-one time with the man in the flesh, so to speak, where you could witness and learn first-hand how these guys had made it;

that all of it was teachable and all you needed to do was change your mindset, train and learn from the pros. For the special (this offer ends at midnight) Today Only Price of $199.

Once on their email radar, rather like the Russian Bride situation before, there was an plethora of offers to wade through. Podcasts, video streams, email courses, even your very own advisor to reach on the end of a phone and by buying into one, you became fair game for all the others, as if they were all in cahoots together, sharing the cash pool created by the legion lonely men, aged 16 to 80(?), desperately looking for a way to sexual Nirvana.

The offers became an avalanche and, as before, it became difficult to work out the wood from the trees. None of the podcasts had a duration to them, so you would sit there feeling boiler-roomed into a one-time only offer of five videos, two podcasts and a phone session with the Main Man to work out why you were such a weak, indecisive individual, get it beaten out of you and so become completely irresistible to the fairer sex, for the criminally reduced price of not $1750, not $1100, not even $600, but $399.. Yes, you heard that right, let me help you to help yourself for just $399- If you sign up right now (what are you waiting for?). If you hit that fat, throbbing, 'Add To Cart' I-want-to-transform-my-life-right-here-and-now-I-want-to-show-my-commitment-I'm-sick-and-tired-of-myself -and-my-hopeless-helpless-future-and-I-can-only-get-out-of-it-by-paying-you-to-help-me button. Who even owned a cart these days?

The thing is, I wanted it. I wanted to hit that glowing 3-D button. I already had my MasterCard out and sitting on the pile of papers beside me. IT wanted me to do it, It was already sold and wanted to send the piffling amount that would transform not only my life, but make It the credit card It had been Waiting To Be all Its plastic life, negotiating hundreds of thousands in five different currencies, all smoothly, noiselessly, effortlessly. A credit to my life.

Jesus wept.

6

Disembarking, I switched on my phone and waited for it to register a new country, a new timezone and locate a friendly connection, then messaged Arif. Four minutes later, he messaged back.

'Welcome to LA. Look for FLAX.'

A little cryptic, but I wouldn't get any more; it was enough to be going on with for now. I didn't feel half as nervous as I thought I might negotiating the long lines for aliens entering the United States. The Officer I had wanted to know why I was there, to which the answer was 'holiday' and that I was going on to Hawaii and then Australia. He then asked where I would be staying and I said the Marmont. I wasn't, I hadn't even worked that out yet, but I liked the idea of it. He stamped my passport and I went through and out into Arrivals, a sea of faces, many holding a variety of placards. One leapt out at me.

The chap holding the FLAX card was more of a chauffeur than a cabbie, peaked cap and all, he insisted on taking my bags, though I kept hold of my knapsack. I was too heavily dressed for the heat of LA, which hit my entire body the moment we walked free of the building.

He took me to a ridiculous black limo, courteously opening the door for me, before putting my case in the back. I spread myself on my second leather seat and looked at the palm trees and sky through the heavily tinted glass, the nodding donkeys of unexpected oil fields greeting my first trip to the US.

The glass between myself and my unknown driver was already up, so I fished my phone out to ring the number Arif had given me. At the same moment, the window infront came down and the driver spoke.

"You have a call, sir."

"I do?"

Over the speaker system, a warm, American voice boomed.

"Hi."

"Hello, is that Sammie?"

"Hey, Tony. Welcome to LA. I trust you had a pleasant trip."

"Yes, thankyou. No mishaps." The air con was already having the desired effect.

"No mishaps.. Well, that's good to hear. And you're in the car now. All good."

"Yes."

"Perfect. Well, sit back, enjoy the ride, take a drink, watch TV, whatever you like and I'll see you in a little while."

"Thankyou.. Umm.. Yes, thankyou.." He hung up.

I didn't fancy a drink, other than water which, after a

little investigation into the cushioned leather cabinets infront of me, I did help myself to. I sniffed my pits, belatedly worried about my appearance and how I was going to present to this mystery man. There was little I could do about it.

LA was truly enormous. We headed into some mountains, a place called Topanga and eventually swung into a ranch, deep in some woods, the tyres silenced by the needle carpet beneath. We approached what I took to be stables and a huge, sprawling wooden building that seemed to go on and on.

As we pulled up, a man dismounted from a horse passing the reins to the stablehand in attendance. He pulled off his gloves, brushing back his thick mop of black hair and shook my hand, leaving me feeling horribly under dressed and shabby at a stroke.

"I'm Sammie. Thankyou for coming so far out of your way. Come through. Would you like some lemonade? Something stronger..?"

"Lemonade sounds great." I said. I was finding it hard to adjust to the shock of stepping in and out of air-conditioned environments... the airport to the car, the car to the house. It was odd, but welcome indeed as the heat was ferocious, even in the shade.

We strolled through to a huge, lavish lounge containing the biggest sofa I'd ever seen, so placed to take in the breathtaking view, out across the valley through the window wall.

"This is quite some place."

"You're very kind. I like to think so. Take a seat."

I did so, still transfixed by the panorama.

"Do you have the ahh..."

"Yes, I'm so sorry, how rude." I immediately dived into my bag, opening the wrong compartment in my fluster, but eventually extracted the drive from its pocket. He made no move to take it, signalling a gloved minion I hadn't spotted.

"This is Davis."

I nodded my hello as Davis took it off me and retreated to plug it into a laptop on a desk in the corner.

"So, how long are you staying?"

A maid circled with a tray, depositing first a mat and then an elegant but large glass at my elbow.

"I'm not exactly sure. I haven't worked it out really, I just needed to get away, but my ticket goes on through Hawaii.."

So you've no idea how long in LA? Where're you staying?"

"I haven't decided. I thought I would get here and decide.. Find somewhere nice, you know?"

He didn't really look anything like Arif, although he was definitely the same race. Whatever that was. He was taller, slimmer and much more refined. Modern chic, I wondered what he did. He turned and looked at the young man bent intently over the laptop, who nodded to him. This seemed to relax Sammie and he was immediately more expansive.

"Well, you must avail yourself of my hospitality. We Americans are famous for it. Do you like candy?"

As he sat, he indicated something I took to be dunes of coke, sitting previously unnoticed on the central glass table. I hesitated a moment. Shit, why not?

I nodded and bent forward to take a line then leant back, expecting it to smack the back of my throat, but it didn't. It slipped in with no bitterness, no bite at all. It was good. Very good. I caught Davis looking at me.

"Where would you like to stay?"

I took a moment to respond, man, it was good.

"I don't really know LA. I mean, I've only heard of a couple of places, like the Marmont and the Beverly Hills Hotel.. But.."

I watched him think for a millisecond, even as I was saying it.

"You want Chateau Marmont? Sure. Why not?" He waved a hand as he said this and Davis started typing behind him.

"No really, I don't mean.."

The same hand stopped me mid-flow.

"Do you know what was on that?" He indicated what I took to mean the drive.

"No."

"No. Ok, but Arif still trusted you to bring it. And you did, right, so that deserves some credit. You've done me a great favour and I don't like being obliged, so.. is that ok with you?"

"Sure."

"Chateau Marmont and we're even, right?"

I nodded.

"Sure. It's very generous of you.."

"Least I can do." He got up abruptly. "Now, if you don't mind, I've got some things to attend to, infact I'm going to take your chauffeur, if that's alright, but Davis here will look after you. Ok, Davis? You'll get him to the Marmont, am I right?"

Davis nodded pleasantly. "Ahh, Yes. Of course. The Marmont. Yes."

"A pleasure meeting you. Your hotel is booked, they'll bill me, so don't worry about a thing. Stay as long as you want. And if you'd like to come to dinner, we're having a few people over, Friday. You got my number, just let me know." Said Sammie.

"Thankyou. I will, thankyou." I got up to shake his cool hand and he evaporated the way we came in. I turned to Davis, who had sunk back into his screen, so I took the opportunity to slug my forgotten lemonade, delivered so noiselessly by the maid. It was outstandingly fresh and bitingly cold. Just beautiful. I'd never tasted lemonade like it. Infact, I questioned every drink of lemonade I'd ever tasted before, as a poor fake next to this.

Well, I wanted change, I'd asked for adventure and I'd surely found it, hadn't I? Even if I didn't quite know what adventure I'd just taken part in. Looking out through the tinted glass across the fury of heat stretching off into the tree covered distance and the city below, I raised a silent glass to myself and my new beginning.

Davis slapping the laptop shut snapped me out of my reverie.

He headed round the table and towards the exit.

"Mr Pesic. Do you mind if we make a detour?" I have to go to work.. It really won't take long.."

He had a distinct Latino accent I rather liked.

"Tony. Call me Tony, please. Not at all. Would you prefer I get a cab?"

"Oh no, that's not what I mean. I just need to drop in for ten minutes, no longer, it's totally on the way."

"Sure, why not."

We climbed into a black SUV, my case already in the back. He was obviously very preoccupied, but I was curious about well, a lot of things.

7

I let Davis get onto the main road before commencing my mini-inquisition.

"How long have you worked for Sammie?"

"Maybe four years, off and on. I don't actually work for him, he hires me from time to time."

"Oh. What do you do?"

"I'm a biochemist."

"Wow. Ok. That was unexpected."

We wound our way back down the hill I'd come up earlier, a very different experience, sitting in the front, so much higher up as we were in the four by four. Everything was bigger, more generous, more showy than in the UK. Mind you, I did have a face full of coke.

"What have you specialised in?"

"Cryonics."

"Do I know what that is?"

He smiled at this. "You might know it as like, cryogenics. But more accurately, it's cryonics."

"Ok. Cool."

"Very. Minus 196 degrees cool."

"Liquid nitrogen, right?"

"That's right. How did you know that?"

I shrugged. I wanted to say 'well educated', but didn't feel I wanted to insult him. Not yet anyway.

"You know about cryonics?"

"No, not at all, beyond the basics." I said.

His eyes were fixed on the curves of the road as we descended into the valley.

"Do you believe it works?" He said.

"What, that you can freeze someone and bring them back to life? No, I guess not. I mean, I believe you can freeze someone, even that you can.. prevent cells from bursting at super-low temps, but not about science bringing anyone back from the dead, no." Perhaps unsurprisingly, one of the many news articles that had leapt out at me in the weeks after my father's passing was on cryogenics, though I struggled to recall too much of it, now I was put on the spot. I looked at Davis to see what impact my summation had on him. I didn't want to say anything out of turn. He paused before answering.

"I'm impressed you have an opinion at all, to be honest. Most people wouldn't be able to have a conversation about it: Know about water expansion under freezing. Are you a chemist? A scientist?"

"No. Not at all. I have a good education.. Naturally curious, is all."

"Yes, you English, you're all dangerously educated, ain't yah?" he laughed. "Well, if you like you can come in and have a look while I just do something..."

"Great."

We pulled into a short driveway signposted 'Vermilion', Davis punched a keypad entry to open the automated gate and we drove into a concrete slipway, coiling steeply under the building to park up. From there, through a secure, sprung door into a short, well-lit corridor and then, once he'd spoken into a microphone-entry final door, into an unexpectedly spacious cavern. It was crammed with stainless steel tanks and miles of piping, the fluorescent air heavy with a strong, industrial hum. Weaving his way though, we approached a cramped desk with a couple of computers and instrumentation on it next to a basketball hoop and fridge, looking decidedly at odds with their surrounds.

"Is this what I think it is?"

"It might be." He replied.

I lost him as he logged into the computer, using the moment to take in my surroundings in greater detail, not sure how I felt about the idea that the horizontal, stainless-steel capsules towards the back wall in all probability, contained bodies. There was another bank with smaller tanks, again all rigged up and some bigger tubes that disappeared through the wall, which presumably piped in the nitrogen, or something. Everything was smothered in dials, heavily insulated tubes and wiring that all fed to a main bank, which presumably then linked to the computer desk, from which one monitored everything.

"Where they can, they like to double up on everything. Sometimes quadruple. So if possible, everything is monitored in analogue and digital. They also have their own generators upstairs. Two, infact. Incase of power failure."

He announced, over the hum.

"This is your place?"

"What? Oh, no, Mr Pesic, I only work here. But they leave me be with my research, you know."

"What's that.. What research?"

"You can't guess?"

"What? Bringing people back to life?"

Davis smiled and waved me over. Cocaine heart thumping in my chest, I walked across to the desk. On his screen, a series of graphs and numbers.

"This is Frank."

"Hello Frank."

"Not the computer, Frank is over there." He indicated a steel egg, about the size of a small fridge across the table from us, set apart from the other ranked containers.

"What's Frank?"

"Frank is.. Well, he's a 'Neuro'.. the severed head I've been working with. That's not his name. I just call him F for Frank."

Oh, I see." I moved around to study the screen. What was evident from one of the graphs was that Frank had gained significantly in temperature over what looked like the past 11 hours. He now stood at almost 38 degrees centigrade.

"So a Neuro is just the head." I whispered.

Davis nodded in reply.

"What are you planning to do?"

"Well, you can see, he's thawed out. The next step was to reintroduce water-based fluid, a blood plasma substitute that the Swiss only fully developed last year, which I've found successfully transports oxygen through the brain capillaries."

"Wow. Ok. So then what?"

"So, then I introduce a blood protein GDF11... it's a single blood protein called 'Creb'."

"Ok." I was worried this was about to turn into a chemistry lesson and I was going to lose the thread, however riveting it might be.

"It's a young blood protein we all have when we're young, but essentially, it excites brain activity, it's being used to delay dementia... even ageing, in people."

"Right."

"Well, then the next bit is what I've been working on. Only it's a bit unorthodox. It might be frowned on by the trade."

"Why? What are you doing?" The mind boggled.

"Well, it takes six hours or so for this plasma mixture to get in properly, so I can access just one area of the brain successfully.."

"Right."

"Then I introduce electricity.. This human brain reboot as I call it, it needs only about 90 millivolts... But, well, what I'm trying to do, what I have evidence of is.. Well, what you would call brain activity."

"Seriously?" I was still whispering, in a hoarse voice. Fearful in the back of my mind that I might offend or disturb one of the residents with what was frankly, pretty disrespectful chat I wouldn't undertake in a churchyard.

"Yuh. But not much. Just ten seconds.. Ten to fifteen, max. Take a look at this."

He went into a folder, pulling up a sample on screen and I watched as he clicked 'play' and the signal jumped a few times and then stopped. I had no idea what I'd just watched.

"So this is a previous Neuro, I called 'Bill'..."

It wasn't much to look at. But if it was as he said it was,

then it was.. well, groundbreaking.

I mean, who in their right minds ever thought that being frozen cryogenically was anything more than a vain waste of a huge amount of money? But if what Davis was showing me was what he said it was, then this was kind of astonishing.

"What d'you think?"

"It's amazing. If it's what you say it is, it's amazing."

"That's not all though. I've been trying to translate that signal. For a while there, I wondered whether it would be possible to translate it into an image, a movie.. but of course, it's an organic electro-chemical thing.. A burst of reconnected synapses. You can't possibly translate that onto a screen... any better than I already did here.."

We looked again at the simple electrical fizzle that represented Bill's last moments repeating across the screen. I couldn't even be sure it was anything more than the electricity Davis was himself jamming into the head, but I wasn't going to say that. Certainly, it didn't view as a single pulse that died out, but a line that drew it's own story, independently of the point where the electricity was evidently introduced.

"So where do you go from here?"

"I wanna plug it into my own brain, to you know, see if I could see anything."

"Jesus. Did it work?"

"No. I.. It doesn't.. I can't.." He failed to finish any of his sentences and petered out, looking disconsolately back at the pulse of Bill on the screen. I felt sorry for him. I couldn't imagine how much work had gone into the discoveries he'd already made up to this point. I also wondered why he was telling it all to me, a complete stranger.

"Why would you share all this with me, Davis? I mean, I'm no scientist. I do get what you're doing, what you're saying it's amazing. It really is, it's pretty damn mind-blowing to be honest, but... I can't help you. I'm not able to help in any way.. I don't know enough. You understand? I mean, I get the rudiments of Cryonics, and the basic science of... what you're doing, don't get me wrong, but..."

"D'you wanna help?"

"What do you mean?"

"You know, in any field, it doesn't matter if it's archaeology, cancer research, the human genome, particle science, always, the weakest component are the people working on it. They're all immature, weak, stupid.. Competitive. You know? I was working on this thing with some guys, a guy and a girl I was at college with. We went through five years together, but in the end, it all ended up about who owned it. But it's not about that, you understand?"

"Yeah, I think so. But.. But what can I do?"

"You're not from here. You aren't a scientist. You're an outsider."

"Sure, but.. Exactly."

"I need a different brain to put this in. I can't do this on my own. I can't put it into the right point in my own brain and activate it and monitor everything... and still be safe, you know? Take care of things after.."

"You want to put that.. stick that... plug Frank's brain into mine, is that it?"

He paused for a second.

"Yeah."

"Jesus."

"I can do it just right, I can make sure everything is ok,

that you're safe, you see?"

I stared at the floor. It was so fucking crazy. But the cocaine washing round my own brain was really pretty stoked by the idea.

"We only get one shot. I can only bring this out one time. Then the head won't do it again. It's a one shot thing. So you can see, it's an expensive time-consuming thing to do. What do you think?"

"How does it work? What would you do?"

I could see the excitement rising in him as he started to explain.

"I have to connect your brain to his with a thin pipe.."

"How? How would you connect us? You mean a needle?"

"Yeah. A fine needle into your cranium, the tube... is filled with plasma, the other end into Frank. We ensure the fluid.. there are no bubbles, right? Optimum temperature... and then a tiny pulse to excite the synapses.."

"You want me to let you stick a needle right into my brain and connect it to a dead man's skull, so fluid can flow freely between the two of us.."

"Your brain fluid needs to mix thoroughly with that of Frank."

"Ok. Let's do it."

It took almost two hours for Davis to even be ready, during which time I took a shower, went to the loo and raided the fridge, before finally returning, ready to take my place on a bed rigged up with heavy leather limb and torso straps and a medical neck and head brace, preventing any movement at all, once it was tightened up.

"I've laid out some more coke, take a couple of lines. It's good."

"Does it help?"

"I find it eases transition between the blood-brain barrier.. Opens the pleasure centres.."

"Quite aside from lowering any inhibitions I might have."

"Quite aside from that, yeah." He grinned.

He moved about as a man possessed, doing everything so fast and efficiently I was afraid he'd cock it up, but I reckoned he was nervous that if he didn't do it now, I might change my mind and scupper everything. Maybe it was the coke coursing through my veins, but the way I saw it, I was possibly about to have the experience of a lifetime. Or die.

"First thing is we need an x-ray. I use this dentist set up.."

I let him get on with it. With no anaesthetic and surrounded by wired pads stuck to the rest of my scalp, I had to keep talking as he slowly inserted the needle in through my suture, but it was in surprisingly quickly. I couldn't even feel it and finally we were ready, Davis had stopped running about and was standing poised over the tap that would join myself and Frank together.

"Ok Tony?"

I don't know what he would have done if I had said 'no, I changed my mind..' Whether he would have stopped everything and reversed it, or not. I couldn't have done anything if he'd gone ahead anyway, completely immobilised as I was and with a steel spike embedded in my skull. What a truly, deeply weird thing to be doing. But I felt good.

"Ok."

"Ok, so I'm going to turn the tap on and then encourage some flow in the tube, ok?"

"Ok."

I heard a small motor turn on and after a moment, I did

feel something odd, a sort of dizzy sensation, though it might have been psychosomatic, or just jet lag.

"Ok, I'm going to engage Frank. Close your eyes. Breathe easy. Not too much.. slow and steady. Relax."

"Ok." I closed my eyes and consciously sank into the bed, though it was odd trying to do so when ones head was so decidedly clamped. But, closing my eyes immediately took me inside myself and my tiredness threatened to overwhelm. It had been quite a long day, after all. I'd managed to snooze for a couple of hours on the flight, but not enough.

I felt a jolt, like someone had forced my eyelids for me, opened a door and let the sunlight flood in. I was in a stables, the ground soft underfoot, the sharp, unmistakable pungence of horse somehow combined itself with the stabbing ache shooting across my locked chest. I spun round to see a stunning woman I'd never seen before, well preserved, but probably in her fifties tumbling towards me, a picture of pain. I realised I was falling, sinking to my knees, to the welcoming floor and she dropped with me, clasping fast to break my fall, my heavy head caught by her breasts as she held me to her shocked heartbeat. Completely calm, I looked up, drinking in her study in desperation, in concern, in love etched on her beautiful face, her tawny hair framing, falling onto one shoulder. She was speaking to me, shouting maybe, but I couldn't hear a thing, just watch her mouth, teeth, her lips forming words, as if in slow motion, separated as if by water, with the sunlight's diffuse, yellow rays lighting her hair in halo, the smell of her perfume, strong light growing, a priceless teardrop splashed hot on my face... and as it rolled away, I was gone with it.

8

Turning on my unforgiving bunk as Lights Out rang out, I rolled back to that first morning waking up; a very different bed, Davis sitting over me.

"You did it, didn't you? You did it."

He was gripping my arm, his face scanning mine, impatient for me to reveal all, to tell him what he already knew.

I recall my bladder being the fullest I can remember it ever being and having to stagger in physical pain to the ensuite toilet before I could engage in anything else, let alone conversation. Not trusting myself, I chose to sit rather than stand, content that no one would ever know, but it was safest.

On the unfamiliar wall opposite was a wooden framed quote.

'*Walk with the dreamers, with the believers, the courageous.*

The cheerful, the planners, the doers, the successful people with their head in the clouds

and their feet on the ground' ~Wilfred Peterson.

I had a splitting headache and whilst I was in the john, Davis prepped a cup of coffee and a glass of iced water, while I rinsed myself under the cold tap, eager to survey my face in the mirror.

I staggered back to bed, not recognising where I was, but neither did I care.

"What day is it?"

"Thursday. You've been asleep for 26-hours, solid."

No wonder my bladder was so full.

"How you feel? You ok?"

"Headache." I feel dry.."

"Drink. Drink this."

He passed the water and I sipped and then gulped it empty, as I realised how good it felt in my throat, then flopped my head back on the pillow.

"You did it, didn't you? It worked."

"Oh, it worked." I nodded.

"Yes! I knew it. Yesss." He slapped my shoulder and did a little fist-pumping jig, beside himself with joy and relief.

"Well done, Davis. You're a genius. I mean that... in the truest sense, a genius. But you're gonna need to do something about the come down.."

Davis sat back down, his head in his hands. I guess I couldn't really know what he must have been through to get to this point, how many years, how many hours, how much disappointment. It was a great moment, only I didn't feel much like celebrating. I didn't feel like doing anything much, really. But even in this state, I felt excited. Jesus. I was part of something truly momentous, of that there was no doubt.

"Davis. What exactly did you do? What did you do to me- in words I can understand. Can you tell me?"

"Without being too much of a geek? Ok, let me see. I chiefly ahh.. I basically connected his Working Memory to your Neocortex: The Fourth Layer of your Neocortex. I flooded you with his memory. You understand?"

It was teetering on the edge of 'no, I didn't really understand', but I guessed it was the best he could do. In the end, it didn't really matter what he did. He could have bounced Frank's brainwaves off Jupiter's third moon using laserbeams, for all I cared. The important thing was he knew exactly what he'd done, he would without any doubt be able to repeat it. No one else really needed to know what he did. All they would want is the results. Bingo.

"It's clumsy." He continued, "There must be more refinements... but you must tell me, what did you see? Did you feel?"

As I sat there, for the first time ever I had that core sensation that I now knew what I wanted to do with my life. And key to that, was that I didn't want to let this man out of my sight.

I related my experience, poorly it has to be said. I was still pretty fuzzy and didn't feel like taking any coffee. But after a hot shower, over a breakfast of three eggs on rye bread toast, I managed to remember more and more detail. The thing he was surprised about was that I couldn't hear anything. I tried to explain that I lived everything... that it was more potent, more poignant, more emotive than anything I had ever done, than any IMAX cinema, any immersive 3-D game, simulator, or rollercoaster. It was complete, like it was me, I was there, living and breathing the experience. It was incredible.

He hopped between being so proud that all his work had paid off at last- that he had been proven right, to the illness of perfectionism- beating on himself for failing to deliver the aural experience on top of everything else and with envy - no not envy, but hurt, hurt that it should be me and not him to first experience the fruits of all of his expertise, all of his endeavour.

From that moment, in our own ways, we both knew we were tied to each other forever.

As he drove me back into town, he related his side of the story; that he'd witnessed not only the telltale signature on the screen, but my own reaction as he'd hit the switch. He could see my body convulse, my arms, hands contract on the gurney, my face open and relax, though my eyes remained shut.

"Like a dog dreaming of rabbits." I laughed.

It all happened quickly and then he was unable to rouse me. He extracted the needle, took all the apparatus off me, but I was dead to the world, so to speak. He couldn't keep me at the lab, so eventually, he pushed me on a gurney to one of their private ambulances, loaded me in the back and brought me home to his place.

He'd then got me through and up the stairs and into the bedroom with the help of his gardener and I'd slept through all of it. He'd finally fallen asleep in the chair next to me, but woken, gone shopping and returned, still with no sign of me stirring.

We resolved that we would tell no one. I would get myself settled in the Marmont, he had quite a few things he also needed to do and then we would meet up for a meal later and work out what happened next. When we parted, I clasped his hand and pulled him in for a hug, finally slapping his back, like we were brothers or something.

Never usually one for a bath, once ensconced in my room, I took a deep, long, floaty soak. It was hard to get my head around all that had happened in the last few days. I then took a nap in the hope of beating the last of my headache, rejoicing in the cool expanse of clean linen, but making sure I first set an alarm, just in case.

Dragged from comatose, I reckoned I'd slept without dreaming. For some reason though, I was desperate for a bible. I pulled open the draws of my bedside table and sure enough, found a copy. The Gospel of John, Chapter Eleven; I stood up and read it out loud to myself slowly, feeling the words in my mouth, hearing them spoken as though it mattered somehow to do so. I needed to get something clear in my head.

'I am the resurrection, and the life. He that believeth in me, though he were dead, yet shall he live: and whosoever liveth and believeth in me shall never die.'

There were two Lazarus's in the bible, one who was a beggar ignored by a rich man, even though he sat outside his house every day, hoping for charity and the other who was brought back from the dead by Jesus.

I scrambled for my screen, impatient with the initial log in to get online for the first time from an unfamiliar IP. Resurrection.. What was it about resurrection? Resurrectionists.. That was it: The term for gravediggers in the nineteenth century. Maybe that was the name. The brand. I rolled these ideas around as I got dressed.

The important thing was to keep Davis onside. I had no idea what his plans were for his discovery, but whatever they were, I needed to be a part of them. The thing staring me in the face, the real difficulty in all of this was that I was more than disposable. I was the first successful guinea pig. Nothing more than that. Eminently binnable.

I wondered what Sammie's role was in all of this. And whether the drive I'd brought over had anything to do with the research- whether it was a crucial element in the resolving of the conundrum Davis had been wrestling. I'd just have to see what I could see.

Davis was an intense type, but also quite an introvert. I reckoned he was easily ensnared to work for people like Sammie.

After a careful examination of the menu, he ordered a salad and some fish. I ordered Champagne and a steak.

"How do you feel? Still bad?"

I realised he meant my headache, which had gone so completely, I'd forgotten about it.

"No I'm great, thanks. Full of beans."

"That's good."

We paused while the sommelier sorted the wine.

"Is that lab part of Sammie's empire? Is that how he makes his money?"

"No.."

"He's nothing to do with it?"

"Not directly."

"What does that mean, not directly?"

Davis visibly squirmed.

"His father was there."

"Was?"

"Well, he still is technically, but.. well.. He's.."

"He's what?

"He's dead."

"Ok, well yes, he would be, I guess. Right?"

"No, I mean, he's really... dead. He was Frank."

"You mean...?"

I hadn't seen that coming.

"Yeah. You see, Sammie didn't really get on with his Pop. He was a stern man, I think. When he passed, he wanted to be preserved, cryonically. All of him. But Sammie didn't want to spend all the money. But he had to do the right thing by the will, so.. So he only froze his head."

"That's much cheaper, right?"

"Yeah, like less than half the cost."

"Which you then unfroze."

"Right."

I could tell there was a lot more to this story.

9

The waiter arrived with our food, positioning it carefully, rotating the plates to offer the best presentation of our food to us. I smiled up at him in thanks, waiting for him to depart.

"Why did you choose him?"

"Well, I have to use Neuros.. There's no point in defrosting whole bodies, when all you want is a head, so it makes sense to use just the Neuros. Ease of access... easy to transport and no one asks questions of a head. I dunno, it just makes sense."

"Yes. But why him? You must have any number of Neuros, right?"

"Well, not so many, actually. Not too many people are preserved, it's a very expensive thing to do. There's other stuff too I won't bore you with, but there aren't that many, really. And Frank is only the sixth.."

I could see he wasn't going to answer this question at all, at least, not yet. It felt weird though, on reflection, that I had witnessed so personally the last moments of Sammie's father, of all people. Presumably something Sammie must never be made aware of. And although the moral aspects of what we had done had been sitting tentatively in the wings, I so far hadn't paid them any heed whatsoever. But the longer they sat there, the bigger they seemed to become. I made headway with my steak.

"What was on that drive I brought over?"

Davis shook his head dismissively.

"Nothing. Nothing important."

"Money? Was it.. Cryptocurrency? Bitcoins or something?"

"No." He chewed, looking at me, weighing whether to let me in, or no. "It's a worm."

"A worm. What a computer virus?"

"Sort of. A worm is a thing that gets into computers and enslaves them. This is a very clever worm, gets in through Windows, closes the door behind itself, wipes its feet, so it can't be traced, or followed in, then enslaves; makes bots of peoples computers."

"What's he trying to do? Take over the world?" I grinned.

"No. But it takes only maybe... 20-30,000 bots to take over any sizeable business. And with a serious worm like this is, you can create a botnet -a sizeable network- control of several hundred thousand computers, maybe a million or more. Government computers, military computers, CIA computers, national grid computers.. Take your pick."

The smile disappeared from my face, along with most of the blood. Time to get back to the matter at hand. I topped his glass with champagne.

"A toast." I said. He raised his glass.

"To life, in all its forms."

"To life." He said. We clinked and drank.

"What do you think you want to do now? Where do you want to go from here?"

"I don't exactly know. I think what's exciting is we know there's still life in there. And if we can find ten seconds, maybe I can find more. Maybe I can bring people back... Right?" He said.

"Right." The Holy Grail. I really hadn't been looking at it in that light. "What I'm thinking is.. Now just go with me for a moment here, but there are any number of people out there who would pay good money to experience what I just experienced. I'm not talking thousands, I'm talking a million.." I shrugged. "Ten.."

He didn't say anything, just took another mouthful, so I did the same. I really couldn't afford to lose my cool here. As far as I could see, it was only Davis I needed to persuade. Sammie was a side-salad to this. It was just me and him. Him and me. Us.

"Now what I can do is I can market this, really low key, right? But to billionaires. We'd only need to hit it a couple of times, right, and we'd both be millionaires." I said.

He wiped his mouth with his napkin, folding it carefully before he replied.

"Yeah, we could do that."

There was a 'but' coming and I felt the need to head him off before he said it.

"Think about it. You said yourself, the scientific world is full of grabbing, egotistical, selfish people, right? I mean how would you monetize this? You tell some corporation about this and they run with it and then where are you? What do you get? How many times in history do you see the inventor, the discoverer, the scientist left penniless and the next guy in the foodchain gets all the dough? All the time it happens. What are you going to do with this? Are you wanting to do a load more research, you know.. perfect it a bit? So do that, but make some money at the same time, right? What's wrong with that? You set yourself up for life. Then if it all goes pearshaped and you get done over, at least you're sorted, right? That's all I'm saying."

I really hadn't meant to go off on one. I hadn't known what I was going to say before I had just said it, but it was only by saying it that it even started to make sense to me; I started to see a way through myself.

"Yes. I see what you're saying." He sounded less certain about his dissent than before.

"There's nothing wrong with looking after yourself. Of course, eventually, everyone is going to need to know, right and you get your name up in lights. Stands to reason. But up til then, we can do this. You see what I'm getting at?"

"So, what you sayin'?"

"I think we need to set up a company, a company with a good name to it. Branding. An offshore account, everything legal and above board, transparent, so you can see and I can see, it's all fifty fifty.." I watched his face flicker. "We both need each other, we're both in it together. I can do the other side of this, run the business, get clients in. You know that's not your forte, right?"

He nodded, a bit crestfallen. I got it right. He knew this was his Achilles heel. I wasn't exactly sure how I was going to do it, but I knew I would be able to take a better stab at it than he ever could. This was good.

"What we calling it? This company?"

"I had a long think about it. I think most of our work is

maybe gonna be online. We need to create a strong online presence on the dark web.." I didn't even know what I was talking about.

"Yes, that makes sense. I can do that."

"Great. Complimentary skills. So what I'm thinking is 'hashtag Lazarus Ten Incorporated'." I scrawled it on my linen napkin as I said it '#Lazarus10 Inc.' He stared at it.

"I like that. I like it a lot."

"Good, huh?" I sat back.

"Awesome." He nodded.

I raised my glass again.

"Hashtag Lazarus Ten."

"Hashtag Lazarus Ten." He smiled. He looked relieved. But not half as relieved as I felt.

10

It was quite upsetting remembering even just the past year from here, buried in my cell. But under 23-hour lockdown, all you had for company was yourself, so it was impossible not to dwell. I figured rather than just stew in it, I'd actually get it down. Not really for me, but I suppose in the belief that enough people were now out there, aware of the story, who might be interested to hear it from my point of view. Well, to be honest I was pushed. There were enough journalists and writers champing at the bit to get the gen, but I didn't feel inclined to give it to them. Why should I? Why should I make them rich, on the back of me? I wouldn't be able to earn a bean from my story one way or the other (not that I'd be around to spend it), that was the law, but at least this way, it was coming from me, not through another mouthpiece, with their interpretation, their slant on everything, or who I was. No judgment.

It took up the hours. Time was all you had in Lake Pen, Arizona. I had been incarcerated in Folsom, in Cali, the original location of my crime. A far cry though from Jonny Cash by the time I arrived. From there, with all the unwelcome attention I was receiving, I was shipped around a fair amount and was expecting Terre Haute in Indiana. That was a serious place.

I was currently standing in the eye of the storm, it was so still. So still, I could watch specks of dust caught in the afternoon sun one after the other, drifting vertically to the floor, some not even spinning on their axis. I had heard of butterflies landing on a man's shirt decorated with red splodges, because a hurricane had stripped the Caribbean island bare of all its flowers, all its colour. They flocked to him there in the eye, when all was flattened around them. As people slowly came out, traumatised, to witness the destruction with disbelieving eyes. But it was a false calm, the furniture about to be rearranged all over again by the other side of the hurricane, 200mph winds ripping everything in its path.

And so it was in Havasu Lake Penitentiary Special Confinement Unit. Here in my concrete box, it was peace personified. Sunlight streamed in every day and all was quiet outside: As though it would always be thus and time stood still. But, beyond the turreted gates a tumult of anger calling for my death and, separated from them, candlelit faces in silent vigil for the end of the death penalty. I had slipped sideways, a pingpong ball in a completely unforeseen political arena.

I was hot. So hot. I didn't see why anyone else needed to be my mouthpiece on the outside. Whatever needed to be said, she was right: I would say myself. And the only way all of it would go away, was if they took me out of the frame once and for all. Then, love me or loathe me, I would have to be laid to rest as a current topic at least and that would be enough for most people irked by me. If things had been different, I would have been on the front of Time magazine. Invited on all the talk shows from here to Mars. Stood for Mayor. As it was, the mere fact that no one could get to me made me even hotter, yet I could go through weeks where I spoke no more than four words in a day. It was so strange.

Terre Haute was selected back in the Nineties as a suitable place to centralise Death Row prisoners, probably because it was relatively centrally located geographically. But more recently, to spread the load, a Special Unit had been constructed by inmates at Lake Pen that currently housed 48 inmates, all lined up for death by lethal injection. I wondered what my parents would have made of me being here. I don't suppose I would have been if they were alive. I wouldn't have taken some of the choices I took, of that I was certain. My father's voice in particular was loud in my head when he was alive, even though I hadn't lived with him for many years. But as soon as he died, I would say within a couple of months, although the voice was still there, I had somehow turned the volume down so much, he was barely audible. I had to concentrate quite hard to hear him again. Something I didn't tend to do at all, if I could help it.

I had been asked a couple of times at some pretty critical junctures whether I regretted what I had done. Sitting here, now, I would say I regretted being caught. Whether I regretted what I had done, the answer wasn't so clear. You see, you only get one shot at life. Too many people devise some sort of living death, myself included. To spend all those years doing a mindless, thankless, pointless job simply to pay a mortgage off. To earn money spent on pointless objects and things especially designed to take ones mind off the fact that one had chosen a sort of death in the first place. And so many billion people had chosen that same path. I was pleased... no, Delighted with myself for stepping out of that self-enslavement. Where day by day, year by year, I was turning the lights out in my building, one by one, floor by floor and perfectly willing to do so. It was horrible. Like some sort of creeping paralysis you'd read about.

No, I had chosen life and I had lived, if only for a fleeting part of my lifespan overall, but I had lived. We all died, after all.

#Lazarus10 became the Burke and Hare for the modern age. Funnily enough it seems that those two, so famous for their grave-robbing antics, didn't actually rob a single grave. Such is the power of spin, the Chinese Whisper of 'legend'. Their first successful sale was a dead body, but one that had died in their company. From there it was a short skip and a jump to actually creating corpses, but none of them actually came out of the ground. Waifs, strays and prostitutes didn't fare so well in their company.

I pressed on with my journal.

I set out to sell a something dressed in smoke and mirrors, in Vegas show, but with the added, inestimable bonus that it actually delivered on all the promise. More. I practiced entrances, speeches, flourishes, in the privacy of my hotel suite. Drew up designs and ideas for the website. It needed to tease, to draw people in. And I needed to aim for those very billionaires who had been-seen-and-done it all. Or thought they had. Between them, it needed to be word of mouth. The website password locked, the password changing daily. Three times daily. I recalled a website idea someone had come up with where, rather than attempting to get everyone to visit, he did the opposite and made it completely exclusive. Only one person could visit it at any one time and they had to pay for the privilege. It went down a storm, a queue of takers. That was the sort of territory we needed to hit.

Yes, I needed to announce myself as a Resurrectionist, offering a one-time only hit.

"I am the Resurrectionist, the life-giver. He that believeth in me, though he were dead, yet shall he live: and whosoever liveth and believeth in me can experience death." They'd go for my English accent as well, I just knew it.

I knew also that my major concern was going to be Davis. I didn't know how many of these experiences he would be willing to sell before he backed out. I had absolutely no idea how much more fiddling and twiddling he would want to do before he felt he had perfected the process. It didn't leave much room. It would be nice to build up to selling them for a million a throw, maybe $50K and then $300K, once we felt truly confident my experience wasn't some flash in the pan. But the way I felt he was, I was going to need to sell them for a million a piece, because there weren't going to be many.

This got me thinking. It didn't matter how much I sold the idea to the first potential client, they were only taking my word for the fact that it worked- that it was any good - and that was a terrible platform from which to start selling anything.

"Does it work? Is it any good?"

"Yes, it does and it's truly amazing... I can't begin to tell you how amazing."

"Whose done it? Who can I talk to?"

"I have and I can tell you..."

"But no one can verify it. No third party..."

"No. Just me. But seriously, it's worth every penny of a million. If I had a mill, I'd spend it on this in a heartbeat."

No, I couldn't see that argument going anywhere. So we needed to rope in say, two people to do it in one go and for a discounted price. Two well-connected people who would do all the legwork for me, bring in new clients overnight. I also needed to talk to some sort of lawyer about nondisclosure, but also indemnity. It really wasn't beyond the realms of possibility that we might have some kind of accident and kill a client on the bed, cause brain damage, or irreversible trauma. We needed to be protected against any comeback. This was America, after all, land of the lawsuit.

But who to ask? And how many goes, how many bites of this cherry did I have to sell? That I didn't know. I didn't even know that Davis hadn't already changed his mind. Or whether he'd agree to doing two people at the same time.

But all I could do was ask.

11

The next day, following a night punctuated by numerous excursions to sit on the loo just to think, I nevertheless felt a lot better about things, more stable, more certain that my way had to be the right way. It was bloody odd though, not to say macabre, that some dead man's brain juices were still swilling around in mine.

I'd decided I was going to ask from the outset that Davis afford us ten 'trips'. Ten trips... and then I would be happy to bow out. I had a strong inkling that he was going to want to do one himself, presumably with me at the controls; I had a strong inkling I was going to want to do another one too. That, plus the kickstarter couple, and that was already four Neuros used up, to very little gain.

So, the maths looked like- two for a million, then two at a million each, two more at five million each, as the word spread, then the final two for $10million a piece, maybe more, depending. By my arithmetic, that made $33million. Factored into that sum were the costs, which would be slight in comparison to the profit, but significant enough not to be overlooked.

For instance, there needed to be a better, streamlined method of ferrying the passengers on this particular journey to a safe house, to rest and recoup. It would need to be an efficient, safe outfit, going to a secluded, upmarket apartment where they could be looked after, undisturbed.

There were the initial set up costs of the website and perhaps a short film. That was a good idea, perhaps to film Davis undergoing the procedure, so that we could definitively illustrate how safe the procedure was: Kill two birds with one stone. And, if he was unwilling to be filmed for professional reasons, it gave me the perfect excuse to undergo the process once again. Calling them 'passengers' was also a good idea.

So. I reckoned, even if we were to lay aside a generous $1m, that should more than cover the relevant legal eagles drawing up necessary waiver documents, the company registration, the offshore account creation, plus foreseeable costs for all the procedures and the minor matter of including the extra staff we would be needing and any unforeseen eventualities, like paying people to look the other way, etc. It would be perfectly possible to hire recognised nurses, who wouldn't need to know what had happened, only that they were looking after some high-net-worth individuals in their recoupment at a private residence, rather than a hotel, where there might be too much potential for unwanted attention or suspicion. And if the clients wished to be delivered to their own homes, once they had been thoroughly briefed and made aware of the come-down, so be it. All this being the case, once the costs were offset and the profits halved, between the two of us, that still earmarked more than $15m as mine.

In the short term though, we were going to need a lump sum to set up the company, the account, the website and draw up the legal documentation, not least between myself and Davis. I needed to show willing and at least offer to stump up half the money for this, if Davis would come up with the other half. I was a bit hazy though as to how much this might be. But we would definitely need all the money from any clients upfront.

It was complicated, but not unmanageable. The other thing I needed to find out was how many heads were actually available. It occurred to me that the briefing beforehand was going to need to be quite thorough, but offer very few guarantees. After all, we would presumably have absolutely no clue how our Neuros had died, or how cogent they were at the time of their passing, so it might be possible someone would get a dud of some sort.. Someone dying after lying in a coma for instance. I wondered whether Davis might be able to gain access to their records; that we might at least be able to do some sort of screening in order to increase the odds of a good trip.

I caught sight of myself in the mirror. I was really buzzing. I hadn't felt this alive since I was eight years old and on my way to see my first Punch & Judy show. The important thing though was to get the next 48-hours right. After that, it got a bit easier, but I wanted to watch over the procedures and make sure nothing went awry. And still, it all lived or died with Davis.

It was hard to appear unconcerned and leave him to do his thing, but I didn't have a choice. The more easy and unconcerned I appeared, the more likely he would be to trust me and bite. The next obstacle infront of me however, was dinner with Sammie. I needed to get ready.

I don't know what it is about hotels, but even if I'm in the most impressive, luxury suite as indeed I was now, I insisted on continuing to live out of my suitcase, unwilling to utilise the free shampoo, or even the wardrobe, let alone the drawers. I had no idea where that came from. It was as though I didn't feel I deserved to be here, or something.

I didn't even need to sort a cab, as Sammie sent a limo to pick me up and waft me to the venue for our eight o'clock. As I approached the entrance, I was straightaway offered what I took to be a champagne cocktail, from the cherry popping in the chilled rose flute and accepted gratefully. Having been quite preoccupied all the way there, upon arrival, I now felt quite nervous. Davis, it turned out, wasn't invited and there were to be six of us. Sammie stepped forward, smiling warmly.

"Tony. Do come in, may I introduce Tony Pesic, from London. This is Natalie, Santa.. Over there is Perry... this is Tony, everyone. Make yourself at home. We're just waiting on one. Santa, why don't you give Tony a quick tour of the place, while we wait on Erin?"

Santa was an impossibly sleek woman in her twenties, who I couldn't help thinking might be a hooker, she was so well put together. However, she was also quite disinterested, which made me change my mind about her immediately. We walked through room after stylish room, the most notable being a rather impressive library and the final one being the games room with obligatory pool table and pinball machine. I guessed it would all look more impressive in the daylight, when the view could also be taken into account. Santa didn't seem to want to be with me, but was well-mannered enough not to show it. However, she remained smilingly silent to my appreciative noises, as we passed by cinema and gym, sauna and steam room. None of it felt like Sammie's taste, very conservative-American, with no hint of Middle-East, but it was easy to be wrong about these things.

"You'll see the stables?"

"Yeah, why not?" I said.

Santa hit a bank of light switches as she opened a side door and we stepped out into the night air, deafened by the cacophony of sex-starved cicadas assaulting our ears. As we rounded the building, a security guard noted our passing, but immediately took his attention off us, so as not to be seen to intrude. Classy. It's what I would have done in his place. Santa's phone pipped discretely and she retrieved it immediately, taking the call with a rueful look, as though it was a call she'd been expecting, too important to ignore. Seeing the stables infront of me, to afford some privacy, I kept walking. The whole yard was lit up with strong lamps, so there was no sense of getting lost. As I reached the door, I glanced back to see Santa had turned away and was engaged in an intense, low dialogue, so pulled on the latch to continue alone, at least until she caught me up.

Despite seeing what I pretty much expected to see, it was nevertheless an impressive set up, with neat rows of immaculate equipment and row upon row of stable door, each no doubt hiding a rather expensive and very well-groomed beast. I wasn't a horsey person at all, but even from the entrance, I could appreciate the amount of money and time that had been expended to make this place happen. As I ventured further in, I was met by the smell and, at the same time, a woman's voice calling my name. I felt disoriented and took another couple of steps inward, thinking perhaps the cocktail I'd demolished quite fast had been spiked, that Davis had lied about Sammie and had told him everything. Again I heard my name, closer this time and from behind me. I veered round clumsily, putting a hand out for any post or support that might happen to be there, half-recognising the face coming towards me as my vision tunnelled, but my head wobbled and then gave up and I was falling to the soft floor, the woman rushing to catch me.

"Hey there, oh God, are you ok?" She said.

I looked up to stare into a face I thought I knew, but I was confused. Fighting the strong urge to black out, I struggled up, dropped back, waited a moment and then struggled up again.

"I'm so sorry.."

"That's ok, are you alright? You looked a little unsure there for a moment.." She smiled, but searched my features for reassurance, holding my arm firmly enough to betray she didn't believe a word I said.

"Yes.. Yes, I'm fine thankyou.. Do I know you?"

"I'm Erin.."

"You know me.."

Then it hit me. She was the woman who had held me when I'd died. When Frank had died. She didn't know me at all, but I knew her. She must have seen a shadow pass across my face and put her other hand out to steady me in case I was going to drop again.

"We'd better get you back inside."

"Yes... Erin.. Yes."

"You have to be on the lookout for rattlesnakes lurking. They like looking for mice in all the straw."

"Oh." I said, brushing straw from my backside.

"You ok with snakes?"

"I'd prefer not to.." I replied.

We made it out of the stables and across the yard unbitten, my eyes now glued to the floor, Erin with her arm in mine, as though a couple, but obviously there incase I decided to collapse again. My mind was doing somersaults. I had recognised the stables at just that moment, when the smell first struck my brain and then, as I had turned, I had been standing in almost exactly the same position as Frank when he had died. It was beyond bizarre. I looked at my companion as we re-entered the house. She looked a little shaken herself, but masked it well.

12

"Are you ok? I didn't mean to frighten you." I said.

"Hey, I'm fine. Totally fine. I was just coming over to get you, as the food is ready. Punishment for being late." Erin replied.

"Not too great a punishment, I hope." I wrestled not to stare, drinking the line of her jaw, the richness of hair and diffident lip.

"No not at all, oh God, I apologise, that came out... all wrong!"

We both laughed and I hoped helped her to recover also from what must have felt to be a bit of a deja vu moment. I caught her perfume again and breathed in til my lungs hurt.

"You have a very refreshing accent." She said.

We were duly seated, myself gratefully adjacent to Erin, who was gracious enough not to mention my little turn in the stables. The food was fine dining, although I didn't really notice it at all. I also elected to stay off any more booze and took to iced, sparkling water instead, something I realised was noted by Sammie, although he didn't say anything either. I couldn't imagine there was much that passed by him unnoticed.

During the meal, I didn't manage to work out who anyone was with any degree of clarity. It didn't seem to matter, but it also felt rude to ask. Having fended off some questions about my life in London, I returned to Erin who was also keeping herself to herself at the tail of the table.

"How do you know Sammie?"

"I was his father's partner, before he passed away."

She looked at me carefully to see how I might take that information.

"Oh, I'm sorry. I didn't mean to pry.."

"No, that's alright. We've always got on well, Sammie and I and he's been very kind about including me. Very kind."

"He seems to be a very generous man." I said.

"Yes, something he got from his mother, I think." She replied, a little hastily, for it seemed she wanted to retract her response immediately having said it.

"How do you know him?"

"We met just a few days ago, I'm a friend of his cousin Arif, in London."

"Ah, ok, that makes sense. I've not met him, but I know of him. How long are you here for?"

"I don't know. I mean, I haven't yet decided. You see, I'm scheduled to fly on to Hawaii, but I can decide when that is. I'd like to stay in LA for a little while though."

"LA is a fun place, if you know good people. Do you have many friends here?"

"Ahh, no, actually, I don't know anyone at all, really."

"You've no one to show you round?" She seemed genuinely shocked.

"No." Looking deeply into her eyes. She appeared quite flustered by this, but I couldn't help myself.

"What are you two conspiring over there? Erin. Own up." Sammie broke in.

"You always bring such interesting people to your parties, Sammie. Can I make a toast?"

"Be my guest."

The company quietened quickly over this exchange between the power players at the table.

"To Mamad."

Sammie immediately stood, dropping his head as he pushed up his glass.

"Mamad" he said. And we all chimed in unison.

"Mamad."

The hubbub returned, more muted than before, but it allowed me to buttonhole Erin again.

"Is that Sammie's father?"

"Yes. He passed five months to the day."

"That's very recent. It must be... very hard for you."

"Yes. Thankyou.."

"Do you live here?"

"Brentwood. Where're you staying?"

"Chateau Marmont."

"Oh, very cool."

"Yeah, it's great. Would you like to meet me for a coffee? One day..?"

My dating gurus would have been proud of me. I was absolutely singleminded and was not going to back down. But it was the most important thing in my life at that moment, the idea that I would never see her again unconscionable.

"Yeah, why not, that would be so cool." As she spoke, she seemed to be communing across the length of the table with Sammie, as though asking either permission or blessing from the man, despite the fact he was deep in conversation with Perry. I would need to be careful; everything was telling me that, but yet I was bent now on a course and couldn't think of anything that would deter me.

The meal devolved into cigars and drinks. I looked at the plump cigars, certain they must be finest Cuban, but having no taste for them. Although right now, I fancied trying one, I was terrified I'd make an absolute idiot of myself in the attempt. It might have to wait til I was on my own.

I found myself near Perry and Natalie. She must have been thirty years his junior, but they were obviously together. A slightly plump man with a bald, shiny head, the fine crown of hair he did have was neatly cropped and he carried himself with a confident air. He and Sammie obviously knew each other well and were matched in status. Erin sidled up unnoticed and spoke close to my ear, making me jump.

"How are you feeling?"

"I'm ok thanks. Sorry for scaring.. Both of us earlier. I usually hope to make a better impression than that."

"Oh, you did ok."

I smelt the alcohol on her breath and latently realised she had infact put away quite a stash of wine during the meal.

Dropping her voice she said "I'm going now. My address is in your pocket."

I resisted immediately diving into my jacket to verify that titbit and managed a small smile instead.

"Very nice to meet you."

"You too, Tony." I kept my eye on her as she bade quiet goodbyes and headed for the door, saving a tiny glance for me as she finally left. My heart leapt.

I stood closer to my host and attempted to look interested.

"I'm sorry, Tony, I was expecting a few more guests, a couple from London and some friends in from Chicago, but they failed to materialise. It must have been a let down for you."

"Not at all Sammie, no. It's been great. And your place is quite spectacular. Your horses are very well looked after.."

"Would your queen approve?"

"Without a doubt." I grinned. He really was incredibly charming, even if I feared him more than any rattlers lurking in the hay.

"Well, that's reassuring. Perry here was very pleased with your delivery, earlier in the week."

"Ah, good. Well, I'm very happy you're happy. And I love the Marmont.."

"Yes, I wondered about that. You took a couple of days getting there, I thought you'd had a change of mind. Was everything ok? Did Davis look after you?"

God. I hadn't even thought of that, but of course, he'd know a great deal more about my movements than I was comfortable with, picking up my tab as he was.

"Davis, yes he's.. He's a good guy. It was all fine. I infact went over to Venice Beach first. I got an email back from some friends of my fathers, so I went and stayed with them."

"Your father passed away recently."

"Yes. As did yours, I'm lead to believe. My condolences."

"Likewise."

I couldn't be sure if my lie had worked or not. I needed to let Davis know of it as soon as possible though, just to head off any potential difficulties.

"What do you make of Santa?"

"Oh, umm, she seems very nice. She's very beautiful.." I was skating around a bit trying to work out what was expected of me in response. I didn't want to come off too lary, but nor did I want to say anything too negative. "...I think she may be having men problems. I hope she's alright." I finished.

"Oh, really? That's not good. I brought her here for you. I'll have a word."

"No, really, that's quite alright. She's very nice, but not my thing.."

"Ok, you sure? It's nothing. I just wanted you to enjoy your stay to the fullest while you were my guest."

"Sammie, that's really very kind of you. Really it is, but.."

"Ok, suit yourself." He smiled.

With Sammie, it was a lined cage, but a cage nonetheless.. it just felt like full ownership or nothing.

"We're gonna sit down to a game of poker. You play?"

"Poker, ah, no I'm afraid I don't." I also wouldn't be able to afford that table, of that I was certain. "I'll take my leave of you then, leave you to it."

"Well ok, then if you're sure. But we'll have you back up here again soon, am I right?"

"That would be great, thankyou. And thankyou for this evening."

"You're welcome."

I made my way out as softly as I could. My car was waiting for me on the driveway and I wondered what to do.

I decided it was best, wherever Brentwood might be, to take this ride back to mine, or at least into town, then get a taxi out, if Erin was still up for guests by then. We made good time to the Marmont and I swung into the foyer, pulling up her recently added digits in my phone as I did so.

"I was wondering where you'd got to."

"I'm on my way.." I said, trying not to sound panicked.

"Good."

A quick stop at the loo and I was back out and into a cab.

Brentwood was a relatively short trip down Santa Monica Boulevard. With perhaps twenty years separating us, I'd no idea what I wanted to say to Erin, or why I felt so impelled to see her even, but I did. I knew I was dancing a dangerous line, I had no idea what her relationship was with Sammie, whether I was playing into his hands even further than I already was. I just knew that nothing was going to stop me finding out.

My phone bleeped. It was Davis. He could wait.

The cab pulled up outside a high-walled, gated residence and I pushed the intercom. There was no further dialogue needed and the steel swept open in welcome.

The door ajar, I entered the gently lit hall, but no sign of Erin.

My nerves jangled. What if it was a set up, Sammie lounging on the sofa, cigar in hand, a disappointed sneer on his face? A voice from above..

"I'm up here."

I mounted the sweeping, semicircular stairs, following the discrete lighting to an open bedroom door. Now expecting to find her in silk lingerie, draped across a massive bed, I was surprised again. She was on the balcony, fully dressed, glass in hand, silhouetted against the city lights. She waved at a second glass waiting for me, the fine condensation making it all the more alluring.

"Beautiful, isn't it?"

"It is." I breathed in the night cityscape, aware I needed to calm everything down.

"You said something earlier. In the stables. Do you remember?"

"You.. know me. Yes, I'm sorry. I didn't mean to.." I faltered.

"Why did you say that? You meant it.. What did you mean?"

I paused for a moment. It didn't feel like a set up. She felt genuine in her questioning. I'd hoped she hadn't noticed, that she'd put it down to my confusion.

"I.. Think I was having a deja vu moment.. Even though I... That was what was so odd."

A deja vu moment. Like you'd been there before.."

"Yeah."

"Been there how?"

"I don't know." I didn't know how much to say. How much to admit to.. Looking at her need right there and then, I wanted to come clean about all of it, but knew it would also be a terrible mistake and one that would only see her hurt and me cast down into Hell. Or worse. But I wanted to communicate something.

"I felt.. It felt like an out of body experience.. Like I had been there, in that spot before and seen you there before, catching me. I know, it doesn't make any sense, I'm sorry."

"No. It makes more sense than you think." She leaned forward and then back again.

I waited for her, afraid if I said anything more I'd blow it.

"Sammie's father died there. Right on that spot, like that.

I caught him as he passed out."

What. Really? Like that?"

"Yes." Tears sprang into her eyes and she turned casually to hide them.

"Wow." I paused for what felt like the right amount of time. "I'm sorry to have put you through that again."

"It's ok, how were you to know? It just...shook me up a bit. You know?"

"Well, yeah, it would. You and me both. Can I offer a toast?"

"Sure."

"To you."

She broke into a smile.

"Why? Why me?"

"I dunno, for being there for both of us when we needed you."

"You're very kind."

We both drank deep.

"But.. So.. Did you feel you weren't yourself? That you were someone else? I mean for you to say you know me, it's like- you must have felt you were there as someone else and I hadn't recognised you, you know? You know what I mean?"

"It kinda felt like... Sometimes these.. inexplicable things happen, right? You hear about them all the time."

"Have you had that kind of thing before?"

"No, never."

"Is that why you were staring at me all through dinner?"

"I felt like.. I felt like I knew you intimately and you... weren't recognising that. It made me panic. I needed to see you again."

"Ok." She took another swig, draining her glass.

"Mamad and I.. We'd known each other a long time. He'd known me since I was pretty young, you know? In the early days, things were good, but as I got older, well, let's just say it got complicated.. I didn't like the degree of control he had over me, but I loved him. He taught me so much about life. Gave me opportunities, we did things I'd never have done otherwise, you know? He created that entire stables for me, for my love of horses."

"Wow."

"So. So I owe him a debt. But we hadn't been lovers for a long time. I loved him though."

"Complicated."

"Exactly. Complicated." She turned to face me.

I leaned in and she didn't pull away. We hovered, our lips apart by the length of an eyelash and then we kissed, quite chaste, enquiring ones at first, but with growing passion as we found each other.

13

I'd never experienced silk sheets before. They were a revelation. I couldn't help stroking them with my forearm as we talked on into dawn.

"So what's it like with Sammie now?"

"Sammie. He's very like his father. I think he reveres me a little.. You know, puts me on a pedestal? Not an easy place to stay. He always kind of used to see me as a sister figure. I think I confused him a lot when I got together with his dad. He was jealous of Mamad spending so much time with me, building the stables and everything.. But, now he's gone, Sammie couldn't be nicer. He's kept the stables, let me keep my horses, the staff, everything exactly as it was. Not quibbled his father's wishes in the will.. I half-expected him to, as Mamad has basically left me almost everything. Not the main house, or the businesses, but a lot of money, two properties, a good amount of stocks and shares. More than

I deserve." She looked at me.

"Do you always make love like that?"

"What d'you mean?"

"It was full on. Intense, you know? I've not felt anything like that before, coming from a man. It was very flattering."

I knew what she meant. I'd had a fire in me. I'd needed to completely possess her, as if I was fighting to regain the intimacy, the intensity I'd experienced with her, the day I died in her arms.

"I dunno.. I find you very attractive."

"Don't get me wrong, it's good, you know, I like it, it was just.. Unexpected." She chuckled.

The light at night can change everything. When you make love with someone, their face can change so greatly, it can be as if you aren't making love to the same person. I didn't feel the same longing, the same need I had felt before we'd consummated, I didn't feel much at all now, as though it could all just be a one night stand. But that was so different to how it had felt prior. I would have endangered everything just to share that, just to get inside her and experience her open up to me. It was weird. But then, how often did you experience what I had experienced? It shouldn't be surprising that there would be some unforeseen consequences or feelings that went along with that.

As I got a cab out of there, I figured it had gone as well as it could have done in the circumstances and hopefully, I'd got away without compromising anything. My life was exhausting.

It felt like I had barely shut my eyes when I was pulled out of my slumber by an insistent knocking at my door. Blearily fixing on my phone clock, I'd had three hours sleep. But the knocking continued, even as my phone lit up on silent. I correctly guessed the person at the door was the same man calling me: Davis.

Pulling myself up, I let him in and again disappeared into the bathroom to stoke some braincells into action. He hadn't caught me at my best.

"I thought we were gonna talk.."

"We were. I'm sorry. I think it must be jet lag. I'm finding it hard to sleep."

"You sure that's all it is?"

"Yeah, don't worry. You want something to eat?" I needed something to create enough space for me to wake up a bit. I dressed sloppily and he guided me past my perfectly good hotel restaurant, into the car and down the road to a pancake house.

I really wasn't ready for a pancake breakfast, but could see the way forward here was to acquiesce as much as possible. He had a tight, strained look about him and evidently needed to get an awful lot off his mind.

"Davis. Are you ok?"

"Yeah, I just thought we would've talked already."

"Sure. I've had a lot going on and I've not been sleeping regularly, I'm sorry." This seemed to work a little bit. "I was out last night at Sammie's? He invited me for a meal, remember? I thought you'd be there infact."

"Oh, ok, no, I don't really know him like that." He nursed a black coffee, whilst I got stuck into a mountain of pancakes and maple syrup.

"Ok, so I've been thinking alot about our little enterprise...." I then made a fist of running the figures and findings I had come up with, now I'd had a chance to re-engage, happy that I had at least made the time to do that, enabling me to recap, as though I knew what I was talking about.

Davis listened, nodding slowly, liking some aspects of my thinking, such as the need for a recuperation house, the professional nurses and the briefing; he'd come to similar conclusions himself. However he added that he would want a full medical team on standby, as that would be the only way we could cover our asses, should the unthinkable happen. He felt that would be the only way we might get anyone to sign our waiver. It seemed a good idea, though I worried that it meant even more people who didn't need to be knowing our business. On the plus side though, this was exactly the sort of thing that would help sell the idea and it was also still within the $1m budget I'd set aside in my mind.

So I offered this amount up as my considered overall budget, plus the idea of ten Neuro's, guaranteed. He went into the tank and I rolled on gently about the idea that we would need two early samplers, who would then sell the journey to their friends, plus my sense that he would himself like a go. He visibly flinched at this notion. It had obviously been on his mind. If I could just maintain this one-step-ahead malarkey..

This proved the deciding factor and he went for it in principle. I could see he had visibly calmed down and was now processing all that I had come up with. I felt I had allayed his fears that I had got cold feet, or had done something untoward behind his back.

At that point I remembered to tell him of my little lie about where I'd been for the first two nights (Venice Beach) and he nodded in agreement that I had done the right thing and that he would also back it up, should it prove necessary.

Over my third coffee, I breathed an inward sigh of relief and pushed a little of my opening pitch idea at him, using the biblical quote.

"That's deep." He said, impressed.

I breezed on, as if it wasn't my last card.

"Do you know any likely lawyers we could approach over this?"

"Yeah, I may do as it happens. I have a guy in Century City, I know Sammie uses him from time to time."

"Is that wise? If he knows Sammie?"

"It's ok, they aren't compadres or anything, there's no allegiances there. Besides, he doesn't even need to know about Frank, right?"

"No one needs to know about Frank." I said.

"Right. But I think you're right, it's going to be quite expensive upfront. Do you have access to any funds?"

"Not like that, no."

"Reckoning the lawyers alone are going to be a million..."

"Really? That much?" I said.

"Yeah. Think about what we're asking them to do. We aren't gonna be able to dress it up any way than what it is. They're gonna need to go in to this with their eyes fully open, or they won't go in at all."

"Jeez. Ok. But I don't have a mill spare, how are we going to find that kind of money? Do you have it?"

"Not really. I'm thinking we want an investor."

This was getting way more complicated- and expensive than I had first thought.

"Would there be any way of getting the lawyer onboard and pay him like.. later? Pay him a nominal fee now, but pay the balance after we've landed our... Fourth client?"

"I dunno..."

"Isn't there another lawyer you know, say that you've known longer, who would trust you?"

"There's a guy dated my sister for a while. Though I don't see him... I'm not even sure he's even still practicing."

"So look into it, at least. I mean, getting an investor, I dunno, that's gonna be pretty difficult, right? And it's another mouth to feed. Another man knowing our business, right?"

"Yeah, I guess, but then if he were one of the guys up front, who got a deal on taking the trip, maybe that works for us, no?" he countered.

I thought for a minute. That wasn't a bad idea. After all, how many billionaires weren't interested in a gamble? But then, he was a third person we'd be cutting up the pie with. It paid not to be greedy though. I dropped my voice as the waitress passed.

"But surely if we got an investor in early, wouldn't he want his trip for free? I mean, we wouldn't even be able to charge him in the first place, right?"

"Maybe so, but I think you may have been light with your math. With your returns."

"Why, what.. what are you thinking?"

"I think we could easily charge ten mill from the start."

"Wow. Really? Ok." I did think -as a Brit and with very little to do with high-net individuals- it did occur to me that I had no idea quite how much one could charge, but then, it was also a unique, once in a lifetime opportunity we were offering, that was for sure.

"So scaling up to... what, by the end..?"

"Fifty."

"Fifty mill? Really?"

"We can't undersell this. Let's face it, like you said, we

want to be set up by the end, right? Anyway, to pull in billionaires, it's gonna need to be expensive. Plus, we're going to have to split this three ways, is my guess."

I was busy doing some mental arithmetic as he said this. He was looking at well over $200m profit which, with an equal split, meant over $70m for each of us. Wiping it first on a couple of thin paper napkins, I stuck out my hand. Davis grinned and took it.

"Ok, you look into lawyers and I'll start drawing up a couple of draft documents to present to them." I said.

"Great. I'll touch base with you in a couple of hours."

He drove me back to the hotel and we parted ways. I'd managed to avoid the whole problem of where I dragged up a few billionaires from, but suspected as we would also be looking for an investor, that he might be able to help. Certainly he was going to be far more plugged into the scene in LA than I ever was; the only one I thought I might know was the one person we needed to avoid at all costs.

But I needed still to keep my wits about me. There were going to be a lot more people involved than I had thought about and the double-cross just loomed bigger by the minute. I needed to get the accounts set up, the agreement with Davis and any third party sorted out first and foremost and then keep a very beady eye on proceedings.

When I got back up to my room, the cleaners were just finishing. I had a stab at drafting an agreement between myself and Davis and drew up a list of bullet points for any potential client, then hit the sack as soon as the cleaners vacated.

When I surfaced, it was gone 5pm and a couple of messages showed on my phone, the first from Davis.

"Am guessing you're asleep.. Look, I'm thinking I've

found us a lawyer. They'll sign on for ten percent of anything we make, but for that, they'll also do it for nothing up front."

Jesus Christ! Ten percent? That worked out at over $20million, the bloodsucking bastards. I suddenly truly understood why people hate lawyers. He continued...

"I know what you're thinking, but this way, we may not even need an investor.. Call me back. I'll send you their deets."

It was true. If these lawyers were worth their salt, they could do not only all the paperwork, but set up the company and the offshore account for that price. That way, we only needed to stump up for the recuperation joint, the staff and medical team for the first takers.

I called him back, but it went through to answer phone.

"Davis.. Tony calling you back, thanks for the update. Yeah, I was out cold, sorry 'bout that. A bit shocked by the lawyer fees- glad I was lying down when I heard your message- but guess I shouldn't be. We also need some sort of escrow account, so any potential passenger can put the money in, then release it to us when they're out the other side... half up front, half after.. Also I forgot to say, there needs -if possible- to be some sort of way to vet the Neuro's, so as far as we can, we know something of the provenance, so we can offer the best possible chance of a good ride, right?. There's no point having someone who passed away in a coma, or whatever, you get me? Speak later."

There was a disdain to American slang, I'd noticed. I'd seen it used before in countless films, but also in the vernacular of the country as a whole, particularly in conflict, where its use somehow carefully extracted any respect for the object of its choice. Sometimes it was merely funny, but other times it seemed calculated, be it for a people, such as the Vietnamese, Mexicans, Iraqi's or Afghans. It was useful... it somehow served to reduce the target to that of a 'thing' and therefore easily negated or disposed of.

I looked up the lawyers online. I didn't glean much, being a high-end bunch was cue for a website overstated in its understatement. But they had a cool address and looked expensive.

We still needed to tot up a budget of initial outgoings and see whether Davis would be able either to fund it all, or else we share the burden. But what was left of my father's nest egg suddenly didn't look so grandiose.

14

Greatly reinvigorated by the amazing shower, I realised with some dismay that I couldn't stay here too much longer. I couldn't lean on Sammie's good will and for a few good reasons.

Firstly, it was rude; it was so expensive and I'd declared I was leaving the country quite soon, when I'd taken him up on his offer. I mean, how long was too long? A week, ok, but beyond two... not so much. And with everything that had happened, I was now looking at months.. My visa gave me just three before I needed to leave anyway.

Secondly, like him, I didn't like to feel obligated and, with this arrangement there was no question I felt owned. Feeling naked, I got dressed.

Thirdly, as and when #Lazarus10 took off, I didn't need to be behoven to anyone, or watched, intentionally or otherwise; I needed to sort out alternative arrangements and probably do so before Davis and I managed to land our first fish. I didn't really know where to look though. I needed somewhere with a little clout; who was to say I wouldn't be entertaining potential clients and where better than a famous hotel? It was all coming back to the money though. Would it be too cheeky to try and put it under expenses? Certainly it was another point I needed to raise with Davis.

The doorbell chimed. Only in America was knocking not going to cut it. I looked through the peephole, then opened it to a bellhop. He had a huge bouquet of flowers and a big grin.

"For me?"

He nodded and entered. Mystified, I let him arrange them in a vase on one of the many table tops as I fished for the wad of dollars I'd taken to keeping as a tip roll, peeling off a tenner. I stared at them for a good few minutes, they really were stunning, although not being roses, tulips, lilies, or daffs, I had no idea what they were, other than huge and overdone, as was the case over here. At a guess, they were from Sammie? Not Arif, he'd never do anything so classy, or gay. Might they be bugged? I guess, if Sammie was going to bug me, he would do so in a far more sophisticated way.. Slave my computer, or come in through my phone. Besides, if I was being tapped, I was already sunk.

I plucked the embossed envelope from its fragrant perch and opened it. Erin: She wanted to see me again, expressing how much she'd enjoyed our evening together. Everyone always said and indeed, I'd witnessed myself, that when you really couldn't be arsed, nine times out of ten, it drove the other party to distraction. It was like, No.3 in 'Ways To Keep Her Interested', on one of my gurus vids. Simply impossible to do if you liked her.

And I had liked being with her, even toyed with the idea that she might well be able to lead me to possible passengers, but never quite been stupid or inebriated enough to believe it. She knew it was a temporary thing, that I was leaving the country some point soon. But it was so dangerous and the best thing to do was draw a line under it. There was no way of ensuring Sammie wouldn't find out, or even whether she would just tell him, but I knew, as sure as eggs is eggs that he wouldn't like it one bit. I stopped for a second, seeking my face out in one of the many mirrors dotted about the place. I'd wanted excitement, hadn't I?

Straightaway, I had performance issues. What if I wasn't able to take her like the possessive stallion I'd been the last outing, consumed as I was by my irrational need to conquer? There was no doubt it would be a totally different prospect; I just didn't feel about her the same way, for sure, even though I did find her attractive... in an older woman kind of way. But she was also sweet natured and seemed genuine. She wasn't someone to discard that was for sure and she'd already proved an invaluable source of intel about Sammie, however, tonight I really needed to focus. Perhaps meet her tomorrow for lunch. She didn't want lunch though. I paused in my messaging. Ok, dinner. But not here, not on Sammie's tab. I'd pump her for information and then fade away.

The doorbell went again. Jesus. It was like a conspiracy. Why would no one let me sleep?

I don't know what I would have done differently if I'd checked the peephole first, probably nothing, but I might have felt fractionally better prepared, as the person facing me when I swung it open was Sammie. Perhaps his ears were burning. I've no idea what my face might have betrayed, but

I did my honest best, standing aside to let him in with a surprised expression papered over the blind terror beneath.

As we both sauntered in, I scrabbled to get any sense of normalcy back, with every artificially slowed breath.

"This is a nice surprise. To what do I owe the pleasure?"

"I just thought I'd come by, see how you were doing. It would be a lie to say I was just in the neighbourhood, but I was feeling a sense of responsibility for your time here. How do you like this?" He indicated the suite.

"It's lovely, it's just... well, look at it." My eye stopped like that of a guilty man on the opened envelope and card left thoughtlessly by the flowers. "..Fantastic. What the Americans do best."

His gaze had followed mine.

"Oh, you've already been making inroads, I see. That's great. Anyone I know?"

He crossed to the flowers and, as I mimed him, I saw with relief that the card would need to be flipped over to be read. My heart was getting the best workout it'd had since the coke.

"What are they?" He touched a petal, his eyes burning a hole in the card, but I was convinced he simply wouldn't allow himself to pick it up. The important thing was for me to leave it exactly where it was. I was conjuring up a lie that they were from my wonderful Venice Beach friends, a welcome or something, but I knew that was a hole I didn't want to dig. I would never be able to create a good enough fake existence, who they were, how I knew them, what they did, where they lived... and anyway, the flowers didn't smell like a welcome, they stank of sex.

"Do you know I have no idea.. I was hoping you could tell me." I laughed.

"Can't help you. I can name a few trees is all. So, do y'have plans, or can I take you out?"

"No plans, though I am still ridiculously tired. I've really not managed my jet lag at all well. I heard it was worse going the other way, going back, but I'm not coping at all."

"I'm sorry to hear that. Would you like me to leave you be..?"

"No, I didn't mean it that way, that was very rude, I meant... No, I think staying awake today and then going to bed at the proper time is probably the best thing I could do, if I'm going to make this work. I'm not used to international travel."

"Ok, if you're sure."

"Yeah, it'll be great. I'm honoured.. You must be a busy man."

"Yes and no. The one thing wealth can do for you is make you appreciate time. Time is the real currency. How you spend it."

"Agreed. I was thinking just that at my father's funeral."

"Yeah, I concur. It's those times when you take stock."

'Concur'? Jesus. This guy was educated. I don't know why that word should frighten me, but then I was so used to the concept that Yanks were anything but erudite. Which was so wrong, really. Besides, he probably wouldn't call himself a true Yank through and through. Thank God I had already dressed. I wouldn't have been able to trust him in this room alone. But he surprised me again.

"I'll head down to the foyer. You freshen up and I'll see you down there."

"Ok, great." God, he had so much class.

The moment the door shut, I ran to the offending card and picked it up. I suddenly didn't know what to do with it. I didn't want to throw it away, but equally didn't want to keep incriminating evidence. Wasn't I supposed to burn it? Only because he seemed to suggest it, I changed again and took the opportunity to clean my teeth. As I did so I had a stern word with myself in the magnifying shaving mirror. I had no reason to be so on edge with the man. As far as he was aware, I'd done absolutely nothing wrong. Nothing at all. Infact, I'd delivered something to him of great worth and done so seamlessly. He was indebted to me and wanted to show me a good time. Now, what I needed to do was come up with a good reason for why I wanted to stay and then gently let him down by taking myself out of the hotel. Which gave me an idea.

I called Davis, praying he would pick up.

"Hey."

"Hey, Davis. Thanks for picking up.. Can you talk?"

"Go ahead."

"Ok, so Sammie just arrived on my doorstep and is taking me out... I don't know where."

"Ok.."

" But what I got to thinking was, well I wasn't meant to be staying in LA more than a couple of days, but now it looks like well, at least a month or two.. But I can't stay here, at the Marmont on his ticket, that wouldn't be right."

"Yeah, I see what you're sayin'."

"So then I thought, I should get out, but still be somewhere quite swanky if I'm to impress clients.. But also, what do I say to him? How do I get out of here and still hang in LA?"

"Ok, so just stay what.. A couple more days, right? About a week is ok.. Then say you wanna go to San Fran.. or Vegas, or somewhere. Go there a coupla days and then when you get back, you can sort yourself out someplace... How's that?"

"Davis -I've said it before- you're a genius. That's a great idea."

"So it'll mean you take a couple days out, but that's ok, it's gonna take the lawyers a while to sort out their end, right? So long as we meet them up beforehand, so they can be getting on with stuff. Do you know anyone? I mean, can you stay with anyone in San Fran?"

" No. I don't know a soul, but driving up the PCH sounds like a plan. Or Vegas. Would I like Vegas?"

"I dunno. D'you gamble? One day there is like a week. Plus, I dunno how much fun it'd be on your own.."

"Never gambled really.. But I like the idea of Vegas. I'll think about it. I have to go, but thanks for taking the time.."

"Not at all. Am I seeing you later?"

"I'm really not sure what Sammie has planned... But either way, let's try and talk. See if you can arrange a meet with those lawyers, either tomorrow lunch, or the day after. For that kinda money, they should jump when we say, right?"

"Right."

Feeling much better about things, I headed down to reception. Sitting on the sofa, Sammie looked the part, completely at home, unlike me.

"Do you need to eat?"He said.

"No, I'm good.."

"Great."

15

The reassuring bucket-seat embrace of a Ferrari 599 rescued us from the raisin-making California sun. With no sign of a chauffeur, Sammie took to the cockpit. I guess if I owned one, I'd wish to experience it too. We powered down Sunset and out onto the 5, heading North. He seemed content to just drive, albeit with somewhere specific in mind, so I was happy to sink into the cool upholstery, speak only when spoken to and enjoy the adventure of being catapulted in a moving icon, with the sun bouncing off the open road before us. Eventually, we pulled off the 99 and headed into a giant's forest.

What he wanted to show me were the immense sequoias. They really were incredible and again, I was surprised by his choices. Why, of all the things he could have picked, would he elect to bring me here? The bole of the tree we stood by was larger than a good-sized house.

"Impressive, huh?"

"Astonishing. I've never seen anything like them. Pictures just don't do it justice."

"Been here so long. And they'll be here long after we've gone."

"No doubt." I said.

I just couldn't get the measure of him. I was constantly expecting him to know something, to turn and accuse, or threaten me, but... nothing. However, it also left me at a loss as to what to talk about. I didn't feel I could question him about what he did, I obviously couldn't talk about the hard drive, I couldn't even talk about what had happened to me recently, or about Davis, or indeed, of Erin. There really didn't feel to be a lot left. Looking directly up at the distant canopy, I breathed in the cool air. My dad would have loved it up here.

"How long have you lived in LA?"

"Twenty two years. I like it. The climate suits, we got the ocean, you know? We can get anywhere from there. Great views. Land of milk and honey."

"You do have a good life. What I've seen of it."

"How about you, Tony. Are you happy?"

"I've been stuck a good while."

"You seem too bright, too switched on to be a security guard. That's for sure. I couldn't work that out when Arif told me. Didn't make sense."

I nodded. It felt a bit like being infront of the headmaster, but not badly so.

"I know I've been coasting a while, not really knowing what I wanted."

"Do you know now?"

"I knew I didn't want to stand still any more. I wanted to

travel a bit.." I needed to be careful. "I didn't get a massive inheritance, but it's allowed me to get off the treadmill and see something of the world."

"I hear yah. It's difficult when you don't know what you want, am I right?"

"Exactly. My mum and dad, they always knew, but.." I shrugged.

"He was a violin maker.. What do they call them..."

"Luthier, a luthier."

"Right. So, hopefully, this trip of yours, maybe you find out what you want. It's never too late, you know. Never too late."

"What did you want to be?"

"Me?" He chuckled and took in the view through the massive trunks before answering. "I always wanted to be a dancer."

"A dancer? What kind?"

"Classical ballet."

"Really?"

"You never guessed, right? Am I right? You would never have guessed that. Not in a million years."

"So why not? Why not ballet?"

"My dad." He got up from his crouched position and started walking again. I figured the conversation over.

"He had a strong personality. Very strong. Dancing wasn't for boys." He continued.

"I see. My dad never really understood me. I think I was a constant source of bemusement... I took no interest in the things he took for granted, like they were food and water. But not to me. He never forced anything on me, I think he was just a bit surprised. It came over as a disappointment. Made me want to go and do something completely different."

"I was groomed to follow him in business. Din't really matter what business, so long as it was business.

And I was ok at it, you know? I was no slouch. But it was never what I wanted. Maybe that made me better at it, I don't know. You know, when you're cool on things, you see them more clearly."

"Exactly."

"You like Erin?" He took the wind out of my lungs.

"Yeah, of course, she's really nice."

"Let's not kid around here. It's just you and me talking. Am I right?" He didn't need to look at my face, his antenna were so acute.

"Sure. I like her."

"Right. I saw the way you looked at her. I knew."

"I'm sorry.. I didn't mean anything by it."

"No, look it's ok. We none of us can.. You know, quell those urges, whatever they may be. Right?"

"Right."

"You're both adults.." He stopped walking again.

"Nothing's happened. Nothing's going to happen. I drank a little too many champagne cocktails. I'm sorry if I was at all overbearing.. Was I rude? Did she say something to you?"

"No, no nothing like that. She didn't need to. I just like to look after her, you know? She's not.. Well she's family, you understand, so I like to take care of her."

"Right. Sure. Of course. I meant no harm."

"She's an attractive woman. There's no reason why a warmblooded man shouldn't feel attracted to her."

I nodded and looked at the floor.

"Shall we go eat?"

"Great."

All the way back to LA. Sammie just wanted to know about what went in to making a violin, shaking his head at the things he found remarkable, asking questions that proved he was listening intently to all I said, not just making polite noises. He seemed genuinely interested. All I knew was I knew less than I thought I did about him before he'd arrived at my door.

Why had I lied about Erin? Was it the right thing to have done? In my bones it felt like it was, but I knew I needed to talk to her and let her know what had transpired. If nothing else, I could say I was defending her honour, her confidentiality, by doing so. I just didn't yet have any kind of handle on what their relationship was. Evidently, she was her own woman and did whatever she wanted to do. Had I taken advantage of her emotional state, so soon after Mamad's death? Some could argue so, but I wouldn't have said so.

Without asking me what I wanted, he stopped at what turned out to be a rather good sushi restaurant, only remembering to ask me whether it was ok once we had been seated by a maitre D who evidently knew Sammie well. I assured him sushi was fine.

Saki was brought without even being requested and Sammie immediately sorted out a couple of slugs.

"Salut."

"Cheers.."

As we waited for the sushi chef to sort out our orders, I thought I would have another go.

"Davis is an interesting guy."

"Yeah, he really is. Super bright. He's another one hides himself."

"How so?"

"Well, he does a bit of computer stuff, but he's a real geek scientist, you know?"

"Right."

"But he seems to be play the perpetual student. Never quite managing to launch. He'll always be owned by someone. I've talked to him about any number of times, but he doesn't seem interested. Maybe you can get some sense out of him."

"Me, well, if you can't, I doubt I can."

"That right there, is your trouble. You're always saying no to things. No to opportunities. That's a real Brit thing, right?"

"I guess it is. Not always though, I brought your hard-drive, right?"

I'd hit a nerve and he immediately looked around concerned someone might have heard.

"I guess you did. Did you never want to know what was on it?"

"Well, at first I thought I did, but then, going through customs, it helped that I didn't. After that, I kinda forgot about it. I mean, if I was meant to know, someone would have told me.."

"That's a good way of looking at things."

"None of my business."

"Right. Like I said, Tony, you're a bright guy. You work out what's important."

Just as the sushi arrived, his phone went. He listened for less than a minute and then got up.

"I have to go, I'm sorry. Take the Ferrari back, I'll get it picked up. Don't worry about this, it's all taken care of. Order what you like.."

"What about your...?"

He waved a hand, already heading for the exit.

Nothing if not unexpected.

I relaxed into my slab, striped generously with immaculate sushi. It really was excellent. Totally fresh, you could taste the Pacific as it melted on your tongue. It seemed criminal not to eat what I could of Sammie's selection too, though by the end, I felt uncomfortably stuffed. All I had to do now was drive a dangerous man's pride and joy somewhere I didn't know, on the wrong side of the road, bolstered by two glasses of strong, hot saki. What could possibly go wrong?

16

Davis collected me at a civilised hour the following morning.

I reflected I actually felt good this morning, probably for the first time since landing. I felt more confident that Sammie knew less than I feared he did and that made me feel a whole lot better about a great many things.

Davis took a moment to search my face.

"Did you sleep?"

"Like the dead."

"You Brits." He smiled. "How it go with Sammie?"

"Really well, I think. In the end, I didn't even need to have the Vegas conversation."

"That's good."

"Yeah, I figure it will just happen, you know organically and it'll all be fine."

"Great."

"So, who are we meeting and how's it gonna go down?"

I could hear myself slipping into some awful pseudo-American, but found myself helpless to stop it.

"Right, yeah, we're meeting Lawrence. He's an Aussie. Maybe South African. I think. Nice guy, wears a suit, knows what he's doing."

"And he's been fully briefed?"

"Yeah, pretty much. Like I say, they needed to go into this thing with their eyes open. I also sent them a bunch of stuff to look over... about the process, you know. I haven't told them everything, like, I don't need them to go off and do it with someone else, but they needed to understand something of the procedure and the associated risks.."

"Sure. Of course."

"So hopefully, they'll hit the ground running and we can sort out... everything we need sorting out."

"Sounds perfect."

The lawyers offices were indeed quite swanky and not at all the reserved affair that the London equivalent might have proved. Having been served coffee, we waited not more than three minutes before being welcomed into a spacious office with expensive, outsized artwork on the walls and a fine view through heavily tinted glass. I'd remembered to wear a jacket, understanding that although a fiercely hot country, whenever I'd encountered air con, I'd found it pretty icy. I was silencing my phone as we walked the few paces to the room, when Davis spoke, under his breath.

"You do the talking, ok?"

We were in the room before I could reply, smelling of clean cologne at an almost toxic level, Lawrence met us at the door, offering seats.

"This is Sophie, she'll be privy to everything, ensuring whatever happens, you get the 24/7 cover you deserve, ok?"

Definitely Australian. We both nodded and took it in turns to shake her elegant, long-fingered hand.

"So this is quite a thing you've got here." He continued, bouncing gently on his exercise ball in place of a chair.

Davis and I looked at each other for a fleeting second and I took a deep breath.

"Yes, we're excited by it."

"And am I right in believing that you have actually undergone it, you've done it...?"

"That's right. It was quite.. Well, it was the most amazing thing I've done. Not having had children or anything, I think it's safe to say that.." I added.

"Well, we've looked through all the info and indeed, even given it to a couple of experts, just to make sure -as far as we can- that you're on-the-level. Certainly all the paperwork, the company, the accounts, the waivers, it's all stuff we can do, although it will take a few days. How soon are you wanting to move with this?"

"Well, we want to go ahead as soon as possible..." I stopped short of telling him my visa concerns.

"Ok, so if you can give us let's say, seven working days.. Ten days max, we can have it all good to go."

That was longer than I'd thought but then, we were looking at quite a lot of different elements.

"So that's the website as well?"

"Yes, that's everything. But I do have one caveat."

"What's that?"

"You're talking of ten Neuros, right and the first two are deals, to get word of mouth.. spread word out there."

I nodded, apprehensive of where he was going to go with it.

"Ok, so what if I'm one of those?"

He watched me, a smile playing, waiting to see how I would react. I suppressed the urge to look at Davis; it being so weak to do so.

"That way, I can know what we're selling is real. But not only that, I can almost guarantee you clients. Look around you. We could hardly rent this place without doing intimate business day-in-day-out with a long list of expensive clients."

Sophie sat passive, relaxed but alert, legs crossed perfectly in a light-grey pencil skirt. I wondered whether they were involved.

"Well, I have a distinct advantage, cos I know this crazy thing actually works. I don't need particularly for you to. Lawyers are a dime a dozen over here. But how about you drop your fee from 10 to 7.5-percent and maybe you have yourself a deal."

"I tell you what Tony, we keep our fee at 10-percent, but, if everything is as you say it is, I guarantee your other pigeon will pay for the honour, rather than freeload. How's that?"

"How much?"

"The guy I've got in mind, he's a Communications whizz. He's also an action junkie, so I reckon, if he likes it, he'll be back for more. But he'll be good for say, 10-mill the first time round. What do you think?"

"Ok, if you bring us our first paying passenger and he understands that the first trip is a one off deal- and he'll have to pay proper price when he comes back... and he brings along another ironclad passenger, you have a deal."

After a short pause, Lawrence nodded, a genuine, toothy grin spreading across his face. He leapt up, coming around the table to shake us both by the hand.

"I'll have Sophie send you our paperwork by end of play

today. Sign that, get it back to us and we'll put the wheels in motion. Soon as you're happy, we'll get started. I'm really looking forward to it. Quite intrigued. You know, it's pretty seldom I actually personally get interested in what our clients are involved in, but this really rocks my boat. Lazarus Ten."

17

Davis hadn't said a word the whole meeting and as we slid down the steps out front, I looked at him for the first time.

"You ok?"

"Yeah. Yeah, I'm more than ok. That went great. Thanks."

"You don't need to thank me."

"I'm no good in those situations. I wouldn't be able to speak, you know? It's what you're good at."

We got into his car.

"Ten days... Longer than we thought." I said.

"Yeah, I was thinking bout that. Rather than San Fran or Vegas, why don't you actually get out of the country, that way, you get a whole new ninety days when you get back."

"That's a good idea. Could go on to Hawaii, spend a week there..."

Davis laughed.

"What?"

"That's not leaving the country, dude."

"Oh. No, it isn't."

"You could go up to Canada, just over the border, that's easiest..."

I don't know why, but Canada didn't really appeal.

"What about the Caribbean? I've always wanted to go there."

"Sure, why not. So long as you get out of the US. Just... Not Cuba, maybe. Where you got in mind?"

"Tobago. Sounds exotic. 'Tobago'. I hear they have turtles hatching on the beach."

"There you go. Take ten days, catch some rays... Where you wanna stay when you get back?"

" How about like a private, hired apartment, rather than a hotel?"

"Sure, good idea. You want me look into it?"

"Yeah great. That would be great."

"Ok, so get yourself off to Tobago and make sure wherever you are, you' got ample wifi."

Switching it off silent, I checked my phone. There was a text from Erin. I needed to firm up my plans with her for the evening. Looked back at the profile Davis represented.

"So, when are you thinking you want to do it?"

He shuffled uncomfortably in his seat.

"You do want to..?"

"Yuh, I just.."

"What?"

"I do. I do, I need to. It's been my life's work, you know?"

He sounded like he was trying to convince himself more than me. I waited.

"I can't stand needles. You know? I just. Can't stand 'em."

"Ah, ok. That makes sense. Yeah, I get you."

"I'll get to it. I will."

I'd not thought him the squeamish type, considering what he'd got himself into, but then, when you were doing it to other people, to objects even, that was a very different thing to actually going through it yourself.

"You just let me know. It's really worth it, Davis, I can't tell you. You've achieved a dream. Don't not do it through fear. We can get a professional nurse in to do the needle, if you prefer."

"It's ok, I'll work up to it. I just.. It'll be ok."

"Ok."

I figured it a good idea to change the subject. "I thought they were going to feed us. You want lunch?"

"Yeah, why not? You like steak?"

"I love steak. You know somewhere?"

"Argentinian. You'll love it."

It was so easy here to eat well, but fail to exercise. Venturing out into the heat was prohibitive, so anywhere you went was achieved by car. Food portions were ridiculous and it was taking time for me to override my upbringing of clearing a plate through inbred politeness. Often, it simply wasn't possible here, but the ensuing waste, covered by a shameful napkin, was obscene.

By the time I got back to the hotel, a couriered parcel from Sophie was awaiting me; a thick sheaf of papers needing signatures in seven places, helpfully marked out by adhesive red arrows, making it easy to simply sign, but I sat down and waded through the entire document, making sure I understood each sentence before moving on.

Content that, as far as I could tell, he wasn't trying to stitch us up in the small print, other than by ensuring that we, #Lazarus10, took all responsibility for our actions, I signed it, then FedExed it on to Davis for his.

So far, so good.

Pleased that was out of the way -at least for now, I went out to the pool and tried to focus on how to deal best with Sammie. I needed to work out a plan that made sense as to why I might go away and come back. Or perhaps I didn't. Surely it was ok for me to do as I pleased, without being answerable to him? There was nothing wrong with going to the Caribbean, then returning and finding alternative digs under my own steam. So, all I needed to do was think of a suitable present as a thankyou for his generosity... and the best person to ask for that was Erin.

Erin was fashionably late, but not too late, as she was picking me up. It seemed to make sense we do it this way round, as she knew the territory and I didn't have a car. She'd made an effort and looked and smelt great.

"Have you done your hair?"

"Oh, you know, I put it up sometimes." She said, pleased I'd noticed.

She took me over to Santa Monica, into a fine and, it appeared, famous restaurant called Rustic Canyon, which served great fish dishes, as well as more adventurous stuff I'd never tried. She sparkled and chatted away and I was content to listen, take in the warm evening air, the lively restaurant crowd and actually feel like I was on holiday for the first time.

"Erin, can I just ask.. does Sammie know we're out together?"

"Would it trouble you if he did? Has he said anything to you?"

"Not directly.. I think he suspects though."

"It's none of his business what I do."

"No, for sure. But.. I didn't know, you know.. etiquette-wise, whether it was a good thing. After all, Mamad passed away relatively recently- I don't mean for you and all that, I just mean for him, if he regarded you as you know..." I tapered off. I really hadn't tackled this at all well, but didn't know how better to try.

"Sammie is another controlling man. He's...complex."

"Yes, I guess that's what I mean.. What I'm picking up on."

"What's he said?"

"Like I say, nothing.. Specific. He's just been very kind to me, I don't wish to be treading on anyone's toes..."

"He doesn't own me. Nobody does."

"Yes, no, of course, that's not what I mean. I'm sorry. I didn't mean to insult you, that's the last thing I wanted. I'm just... trying to do the right thing. I like being with you.."

She'd stopped eating and was looking really upset.

"The thing is, I'm planning on going away for a week or so, to Tobago.. And I was wondering if you'd like to come with me..."

She looked up, hope threatening the corner of her mouth, unsure whether I meant it.

"I was just afraid.. Well, to be honest, I am afraid of Sammie, there's no two ways about it. I just.. I just wasn't sure as I say what the etiquette was around this. I like you, I'd like to spend more time with you, but.. I guess I'd be uncomfortable if Sammie wasn't happy with it, for whatever reason, or failing that, that he would actually need to know about it."

"He wouldn't need to know.."

"Ok, great. So.. Are you busy?"

"Nothing that can't be changed." She said, the smile growing to a grin.

"Would you like to come with?"

"I'd love to. I've never been. Oh my God, are you sure? You're not just saying that? I mean, I've been to St Kitts, before, but... Oh, God, I adore the Carib."

"Well.. Great. Eat up before it gets cold."

She dived back into her John Dory with renewed enthusiasm.

And I was going to Tobago with Erin. How on Earth had that happened?

What it did mean was that everything got upgraded. I had expected to go economy, having sourced a budget hotel somewhere on the island.

Erin didn't do economy. And the hotel was a triple-fine, upmarket, coastal residence with sea views and access straight onto the beach. To give her her due, she didn't expect me to pay for it all. I bought the tickets and she paid for the hotel. Travelling First was a new experience and I understood why people who could afford it, did it. She'd needed some persuading not to hire a private jet, saying 'the wait at the airport was a complete waste of time and why would anyone want to?' This on top of the fact that it was impossible to fly direct. We could have done it and she would have paid, but I just couldn't. I knew I would have been uncomfortable and then felt obligated, somehow. I just didn't have that confidence in the relationship.

She brought far less luggage than I feared, but insisted on her own pillow, which she hugged in the limo, snuggled up to on the flight and favoured in place of the excellent hotel ones. I couldn't determine whether it was some kind of security blanket or not.

18

Funny how, when something's taken away, you really yearn for it. Something had shifted in me, even by then, although I don't think I consciously knew it. Was it from the brain matter of another squirted into mine, or purely the result, the impact of undergoing it, on my own consciousness? I don't know. Perhaps a combination of the two. But when I think of freedom, of what freedom is, of life and living, I quite often think about several moments that happened on that same short vacation to Tobago with Erin.

A good part of me felt I was leaving a great deal to trust. It was only as I sat on the plane, waiting on the apron for take-off that I became aware I was removing myself very much from the action. I would need to make sure I went through all the lawyers paperwork with a fine tooth comb, as and when it materialised.

The second day we were there and Erin had signed me up to learn Scuba with my own private tutor, that I might join her on a few dives over the ensuing days. Lessons started in a pool, which at first seemed a bit insulting, until I found out I was completely incapable of breathing in and out of my mouth. As I stood in the pool, my head shoved below the water line, a mushroom of panic blew up from my gut as I tried to breathe, finally bursting up, coughing and spluttering, grateful my feet at least were grounded in just 4ft of water. It took five days. Longer than anyone else had ever taken, before I eventually mastered the concept of breathing solely through my mouthpiece, rather than my nose and I was finally allowed to try things in the ocean.

Erin was sweet and patient, but couldn't stop herself from a little ribbing at my expense. In those long days spent in the pool, at first she was concerned, but as the days wore on she took to reading on a lounger and then ventured further afield, taking in shopping trips while she waited for me to pull it together. She did also help with the extensive theory and we lay in bed testing each other. When we finally went on our first undersea expedition, it transpired I was not great at conserving my limited air supply and we had to curtail our planned excursion, having burned through my tank far too fast. I had got overwhelmed by this whole new expanse, uncharted territory, where anything could happen. I kept looking up at the surface, not believing where I was. Blue, as far as the eye could see, in any direction. The concept of being in control remained with you. You could decide you were in control, breathe normally and swim, or you could realise you were insignificant in the grand scheme of things: Whether you lived or died made no impact whatsoever on the machinations of the rest of the planet, of the galaxy, the universe. The concept of control became a choice and it was desperately important you made the right choice, 60, 70ft underwater. It blew my mind.

The next day, I made the fatal error of eating kedgeree for breakfast and promptly brought it up 26metres down. It was quite an experience throwing up underwater, trying not to panic, trying think before sucking anything in that it was air, not vomit and not water. Around me, the contents of my stomach were floating about, attracting all sorts of fish to the unexpected brunch. Beneath, diamond shapes betrayed the many Southern Stingrays buried just under the sand. And, despite the terror, no sharks, but also no turtles. Although I had my PADI Open Water certificate, I really wasn't sure how much I'd be using it in future.

But Erin was delighted with my achievement, in fact she was very happy to be there in general and better company than I'd imagined. Lying in late one morning, she came in, exhorting me by bouncing the mattress to get out of bed immediately. As soon as I had some shorts on, she tugged me out of the patio door. Our room opened straight out onto Turtle Beach and, sure enough just twenty yards from our back door, a tiny baby turtle lay in a small turmoil in the white sand, as though someone had come in the night to dig up a sea-chest and not bothered to smooth it all over after. On it's back, the tiny toy thing looked dead, presumably baked in its shell by the searing late morning heat. But, as we stood there looking down, it twitched a fin, just faintly. Bending down, I picked it up carefully, taking a good chunk of sand underneath it, worried that using my hands directly on its skin might somehow cause damage, transfer scent, or something. We went the short distance across scorching sand, what must have been a sand-dunes

Kalahari to the poor creature, to the water. The whole area covered with the telltale tracks of the hundred tiny reptiles that must successfully have negotiated the journey under cover of night.

I put our new young friend into the crystal shallows, the crusted sand dropping away to reveal a perfect turtle in miniature, incredible markings on the shell. Sure enough, on touching the cool water, the fellow soon roused and then, buffeted by the low surf, started swimming determinedly out to sea. Erin was over the moon, hugging me in her relief at saving the young life. In all the immediacy and excitement, we'd forgotten to take a picture. I wondered how it might fare doing this in daytime; whether it would get picked off by some gull or reef shark lurking in deeper waters, but elected not to share my concerns with Erin.

"What was it, do you think?"

Recalling the inflight magazine "A leatherback, I think that's the local species."

That afternoon we ate at a celebrated local restaurant, the tables of which were spread on platforms in the branches of an enormous, sprawling and ancient tree. The view was fabulous and we were joined by a Robin-sized bird, evidently used to diners and quite forward about being included in the feast. We tucked into the best lobster dinner I'd ever had, the succulent flesh perfectly seasoned with herbs and spices; no chilli, just delicate flavours I'd never experienced before, complementing rather than drowning the sweet meat.

Only ten hours and a million miles away. I would give anything to have that meal all over again.

As we made our way out, a fisherman arrived on a bicycle, two impressive looking barracudas, strung by their gills, hung from the handlebars.

I stopped Erin and turned back to the kitchen as he walked his catch in.

"Are those on this evening's menu?" I enquired.

"Yes, why?"

"I'd like to book a table."

From there to Angel Falls, which proved quite a walk from the carpark but, once we'd traipsed through the forest, revealed themselves as really worthwhile. Erin was an excellent companion, not afraid of the silence, content to walk and think, but still remain company.

Standing under the waterfall, my back being pounded almost but not quite to the point of pain, was one of the most invigorating massages I'd ever had; the cool, fresh water so welcome after the full sweat of the long walk there.

"Thankyou for bringing me here. I never would have come if you hadn't brought me."

"I'm really pleased you're here. It's somewhere I've always wanted to come, I don't know why. But I'm glad you're here too." I said.

The sex was very different from that first time. I had to sort of approach it from a different angle in my head. I didn't have the same all consuming urgency. It was like the first time, I'd been off my head on drugs and now I had to discover her for the first time. All over a more tentative, less bull-in-a-china-shop affair.

But Erin was cool with it. She seemed genuinely happy to be together, which made it all easier than I'd worried it might be. The fourth time we had sex, she wept into my neck as she came.

"I'm sorry, I'm so sorry.."

"You ok?"

"Hold me."

The sun, the sea, the sex and the Scuba were proving great for my frame of mind. I felt healthy, happy and truly on holiday. The previous pressures of Lazarus Ten had completely prevented me from relaxing, so it was with slight annoyance that the first email came from Sophie, with documents requiring my attention. I'd not told Erin anything, how could I, really? But I needed to take several hours out to attend to business and was poor company for the rest of the day, even though she was too polite to ask why.

"I'll have some business stuff to attend to in the coming days, I'm sorry. I'll have to do it though, so bear with me. Don't be afraid to take yourself off, diving or whatever. I'd only hold you back anyway."

"That's ok. Do whatever you have to."

I had to avail myself of the hotel Business Centre such as it was, to print off documents, sign and scan them to email back. It wasn't a great set up, but they soon got used to me and we worked out a system. I'd have much preferred to forget about everything; address it all once I returned, but figured if it was important enough for them to be emailing, the least I could do was get it back to them as soon as I could.

The other thing that happened, that I think back to more than I ever believed I would at the time, occurred on the last full day of our trip. I was driving on a main stretch of road not far from the Dwight Yorke Stadium, approaching dusk. As we went down a hill, the road cutting through dense rainforest unnecessarily wide, I overtook a slower lorry on my inside. From a rapidly closing distance, there appeared to be a branch in the middle of the road, quite sizeable, but I judged it not big enough to damage the car, however, as we approached it, I had the dreadful sense that it was infact a large snake and not a branch at all. Swerving at the last second, I attempted to avoid it, but feared I'd caught either it's head or tail.. Not sure which direction it was travelling in with the poor light. I thought for a moment, looking desperately in the mirror at the dark squiggle receding from view and then, at the bottom of the hill, aware of traffic, but relieved to be driving on the left, pulled a u-turn.

"What is it?"

"I think it's a snake, a big one. I gotta go back.. Oh, I hope I didn't kill it."

"Oh my God, really? A snake? Are you sure? It was big.."

I drove slowly back up the other side, scanning the tarmac. Sure enough, it was and by the looks of things, I had missed it. It had traversed the road surprisingly quickly. Grabbing the camera from the footwell, I jumped out. It was beautiful, with clear, dark, diamond-pattern markings on it's back, moving quite quickly for the sanctuary of the dense grass beneath the tree line at the side of the road.

Having taken as many pictures as I could, first from the side and then, as I felt more confident, by standing over it and letting it pass between my legs, I finally watched its tail disappear into the temporary hole it had carved in the curtain of dense grass. The heavy, humid air of the rainforest, laden with a million timeless secrets filled my lungs and I stood there motionless for a moment, taking it all in. These forests must be truly ancient, their majesty entirely lost on you when you simply drove past them, on the way to somewhere else.

Erin stayed in the car. She had no enthusiasm for rainforests, foreign roads at dusk, or large, tropical snakes, whether they proved poisonous or not. Knowing she must be fretting, I reluctantly turned and headed back to the car, all sign of the magnificent beast long gone.

"I can't believe you cared so much about a snake." She shivered.

"I really didn't want to think I killed it. I thought I'd just caught it with the wheel... That would have been awful."

"But it's a snake."

"It's still a life.." I turned the car around again to continue our interrupted journey.

"No, I like that you care, I just didn't think... You didn't have to go out there and stand over it. What if it had bit you?"

"It's a python, a constrictor. They aren't venomous." Even as I said this, I reflected they could probably still deliver a nasty bite.

"How d'you know? When did you become the herpetologist?"

I did a double take and she enjoyed my surprise.

"I could tell by the shape of the head.."

"Like I said.. I thought you were in Security."

"I'm amazed it made it across the road."

"Those woods gimme the creeps."

Why did I care so much about the snake? Would I have cared as much before? Would I have made such a big deal about it? I don't know. But sitting here, I go back to that snake, that forest, over and over.

That last night in our beach residence, for some reason my mind was full of Mamad.

"Why did you go with Mamad? In the first place, I mean?"

"I don't know, he was a real man, you know and someone I respected. He had alot of charisma, more than anyone I knew, of my own age I mean.."

"Were you looking for a father figure?"

"Oh my God, What kinda question is that to ask a girl?"

"Sorry.."

"It's ok. I'll answer if I can." She thought for a moment, pouring herself a Cognac before answering. "Isn't every girl trying to marry her father?"

"Was he like you dad?"

"Oh, not at all, nothing like him. At. All. Dad was absent. He was a drinker and a womaniser, he wasn't around much at all when I was young. It was all my mom."

"So that's a 'yes' rather than what you just said.."

"Yes, well, perhaps I was looking for some kind of idealised father figure, rather than my actual dad."

"Ok. So he was the most important man in your life... he's all you ever dated?"

"I dated other guys, my own age when I was younger, you know, 19 whatever, but they never lasted. I spent long periods on my own. I fell in love with one guy, broke my heart, but he was a player, he never loved me. I suppose he was most like my dad. Unobtainable, you know."

"Then you were alone for a while."

"Yeah. I mean, I had fun, but no one serious. I had a full life I was always doing something, I got really involved in horses, you know, working in stables. So through them I met Mamad and then Sammie. Oh God, he had some fine horses. The first time I saw him, he was on this massive stallion that saw a snake and bolted and he held on to it, he dislocated his shoulder hitting a low branch, but he stayed on the horse and got him under control. Never seen anything like it, that mastery... Confidence. Quite the introduction. I mean, what's not to like?"

"Right."

"He was mature, not a silly little boy. He really looked after the horses, understood them... and his staff, always kind to them, generous. He was so generous. So I started riding his horses and he gifted me Belmont for my 20th birthday. Then, for my 21st, he drew up these plans to have a whole new stables built. Well, it's very appealing, all that, you know? Just for you? And he was never pushy. I mean, I always knew he wanted me, but he never did anything creepy. He was just patient and lovely and kind and.. Then it just happened, you know. I sort of worried about Sammie and how he would take it. Cos I wasn't ever going to replace his mom, you know, but also he'd made it clear he was interested. I could never work out though if he liked me, or if he was just running some kind of sick competition with his dad.. You know, trying to win the prize. It never felt that way with Mamad though. So I chose Mamad."

"How long did it last? Like that..?"

"I don't know. I've always loved him. I don't ever remember not loving him, he was easy to love, but.. and respect. I respected him hugely. But, looking back, I'm not sure I was ever In Love with him, you know? It's a different thing. I don't regret a thing, don't get me wrong. He was hugely good for me, a really good influence, calming, intelligent, so well-read too. He has a great library, have you seen it? But in the end.. You won't tell anyone I've said anything will you? I wouldn't wish for... to get back to the wrong ears..."

"Sure, of course. Goes without saying." I waited.

"Well, in the end, I found him quite controlling. He was always great if things were going his way, but the sun soon went out if it didn't. In the end, I realised I was quite scared of him."

"Sammie's like that. I do respect him, but I'm pretty scared of him." I agreed.

"I know what you mean. I think he has less humanity than his father."

"How did Mamad make his money?"

"I don't know. I never really thought to find out at the time, but I think, looking back, he wasn't the straight businessman I took him for. He only showed what he wanted me to see."

"And Sammie?"

"Sammie's worse. I've no idea... Oh God, you mustn't repeat this, you promise?"

"I promise."

The following morning as we packed up and left our haven, although nothing was said, something had changed between us. I felt a bond that hadn't been there before. As if we'd both come out on this trip in the mindset that we were just going to have a good time, whatever shape that might take. But now, something was different. If anything, it made it all even more unsettling, not less.

Ten hours to San Fran and then the short hop back down to LA.

On the plane we kept it light, chatting intermittently about places we'd been and places we wanted to go, whilst my mind turned to more pressing questions, like what I needed to do once I landed.

If I was going to make a fist of pitching this enterprise, I needed to come up with a better handle than Pesic. I wasn't sure what though. And I also needed to do a little insurance, cover my arse, although I hadn't determined quite what shape that might take either.

Things moved pretty fast the moment I got back.

19

Davis had been busy, arranging an apartment for me in Santa Monica, not too far from the lab, but also on the same block as the apartment he'd sorted as the 'safe house' as I'd come to call it. By his dismissive snort when I asked him about the costs, I assumed it was all to come out of the budget. It wasn't too shabby either, with a pool and a flamboyant new purple Merc parked outside the garage.

And #Lazarus10 was born. Davis and Peso. The modern day Burke and Hare.

Lawrence wasn't wasting any time. The moment the last pieces of the paper jigsaw had been shuffled into place, he was champing at the bit to get strapped onto our dead man's gurney, clamped into the head harness and fed the lethal injection. Davis didn't seem to be in a hurry to go next, but busied himself locating and lining up Neuros, fine-tuning the process and streamlining the aftercare procedure for getting people in and out of the lab with the minimum of fuss.

It was odd being there as an interested observer, following Davis through the process, making copious notes as I did so, nervous that I forget anything, as all of it was crucial. I couldn't imagine what it would be like to be a surgeon, carrying that weight of responsibility every day. The bit that really concerned me was what I would need to do after Davis would be out for the count and so unable to advise me, once it was my turn to be at the helm. He really knew his stuff and it was hard for me to keep up. He'd got used to minimising the tech speak, but there was still a huge amount of info to take in. I needed a YouTube vid.

The other nervy part was the insertion of the needle. It needed to go in to the perfect depth, within a tenth of a millimetre give or take. According to the brain and skull of the passenger, it would differ slightly with everyone and could only reliably be determined by x-ray. This being achieved by using the dentist's rig, but instead of the jaw, aimed at the skull itself. Lawrence was unconcerned on that level, just enthralled by it all, by the anticipation and adventure of it all. Perhaps he had greater confidence than I had, secure in the knowledge that a full medical team sat in the next room, ready to leap in if anything untoward happened. But then, the coke also had a large part to play. It'd be a very different proposition when sober. If anything, Davis seemed more nervous, more concerned than Lawrence, this time round. Certainly he was more jumpy than he'd been with me.

Neuro 'George' had died from a free-diving accident, drowning at sea. But, because he was also a millionaire, he'd been flown by helicopter to the mainland, the procedure of his cryonic freezing already in process, even as he was choppered home.

I wondered whether drowning and the cut of oxygen to the brain was reason enough to make George a bad choice, but Davis was adamant it would work. What did I know? Sure enough, as Davis executed the final procedure and Lawrence went under, the computer betrayed a telltale scrawl.

Considering my first experience of it all, this was terribly boring in comparison. We just had to cater for an inert body. Ten seconds soon came and went, although in this case it was nearer twelve seconds and then it was all about extracting the needle, anaesthetising whilst stemming any blood flow, keeping him warm and secure, then getting him out and off to the safe house as efficiently as possible. I guessed, if Sophie had been involved with him, she would have been present, but was notable only by her absence.

The following day, we were summonsed by the hired help, notifying us that he was conscious, if groggy and wanted to see us. When I arrived, I was surprised to find Davis and Sophie already there, as I had such a short distance to travel. I realised Davis must have been there quite some time and he looked tired. But it was good he was spending so much time and effort in caring for our passengers. It boded well.

Unlike me, Lawrence had actually wet the bed in his sleep, although, as only an Aussie could be, he appeared rather proud of the fact.

We cleared the room and commenced the debrief, just myself and Davis.

"I felt a cold spreading through my skull, like fingers. I felt myself lying on a deck, remembering floating, replaying what had just happened to me.. I couldn't be sure at first whether that was just drugs, or something. But it was like someone had turned a blue light on, I was in the sea, I didn't have enough air in my lungs.. all I could do was think about sharks. I was looking around into the blue and all I could think was that a shark could come out of the deep and take me and there would be absolutely nothing I could do about it. It was just terrifying. That was my total biggest fear, a huge shark snaking up towards me from the depths. A bit before, my chest was in such pain, I needed to breathe, the feeling of needing to take in a bucketful of air, it was excruciating, it was like, I needed to get to the surface to breathe, I knew that, but my lungs had overridden any sense... they were going to breathe anyway, whether I liked it or not and so they did, I just sucked in this huge lungful of water and the moment it hit my throat, I had choked, but all I did was kind of cough a tiny bit but then just suck in more water.. And then everything stopped and... I was lying there, remembering, playing back in my mind's eye what I had just done.. Someone was tossing me about, crushing my chest, I was on my side, throwing water out.. The reason why it had all gone so wrong. I was looking at my arm, floating next to me and it changed infront of my eyes into a woman running in snow, in a snow-covered field and she fell over she was laughing so much.. Just her face... and the snow whited her out.. Just blanked everything white and I felt this amazing sense of... euphoria. Of weightless peace. Jeez.. That's it really. But the words don't.. don't do it all justice. I mean, I was really there."

Somewhere in there, Davis had taken hold of his hand. The spell broken, he checked Lawrence's eyes and the bandaged spot where the needle had gone in. Despite this, it was clear Davis had been moved to tears.

There was no doubting it was powerful stuff. Lawrence

looked drained, totally spent but ecstatic, like he'd run a two-hour marathon.

"Davis. I'm telling you, man, this is the fucking bomb."

Lawrence proved a happy and willing guineapig, going through the aftercare, he made helpful suggestions to improve the service and, like me, seemed to be carrying no adverse affects from the trip. Certainly, he was a willing advocate of the whole enterprise and it wasn't long before we were sitting in his offices with Clovis, a very average-looking fifty-something, fat American with loads of hair, who'd made his billions in mobile communications. I took an instant dislike to him, not because of this, but because he seemed to have no interest beyond what he could get. A high-minded stance perhaps, in view of my situation now.

He'd got involved with Lawrence a couple of years ago when he'd nearly bought an NFL football team, but it had fallen through at the last minute. Having leered once already at Sophie, he grabbed her arse and suggested they go out and get to know each other, in full view of myself and Lawrence. She handled it really well, no doubt not the first time it must have happened.

As Lawrence had suggested, Clovis was good for $10m and in doing so, officially got the ball rolling in terms of #Lazarus Ten being a going concern. With no interest either in the paperwork or risks associated with the procedure, he just needed it to happen on a Friday afternoon, for whatever reason.

As soon as the meeting adjourned and Davis occupying Lawrence, I sidled up to Sophie, accompanying her down the corridor.

"Are you ok? I feel the need to apologise, that was horrible."

"What? Oh, no really, I'm fine. You get used to it. Hazard of the job."

"Yeah, but it's not good. Look, if you want this guy sidelined.. out of it, I'm happy to do that."

She stopped in her tracks "You'd do that? For grabbing my ass, you'd do that?"

"Yeah. Look the way I see it, what we've got is gold. Better than gold. There's plenty of guys, plenty of Clovis's out there lining up to do this. We don't have to take him. Not if we don't want."

"Mr Pesic, that's a really kind thing. I'm really touched. Really I am. But you don't need to pull out of this deal for my sake, really.. it's nothing. But thank you. Means alot to me. Really it does." With a final smile and a fleeting hand on my arm, she turned and walked on.

"So we go ahead with him.." I said, to her departing back.

"Yeah. Go ahead with him, but Do Not Resuscitate if he passes out on the table."

I chuckled. There was a reason why she was where she was. I liked her.

20

Davis had managed to sort out a workable M.O. through the cryonics network. It was a small world once you got there; everyone knew everyone. When word got out during his PhD that he might well be making inroads into the last key piece of the jigsaw, the Holy Grail of bringing people back, the various few cryonics companies were falling over backwards to help. This meant that getting Neuros was significantly easier than he had previously thought.

To all outward appearances, all he was doing was running tests, then returning their Neuro intact a few days later. Any tests they may have run subsequently would betray no change in the Neuro status, no noticeable damage, no deterioration. He didn't even need to tell them he had completely defrosted the head and 'rebaked' it, as he called it. His standing in this narrowest of scientific spheres was unimpeachable.

This in turn opened up the possibilities in terms of

spreading the net wide to find Neuros likely to have an appealing journey, although information on them remained sketchy and often entailed further research into the exact circumstances of their death, this intel not being readily available with the Neuro itself, which was usually only supplied with age, sex, date and medical cause of death. It was also exceedingly difficult to find females; it was easier infact to find dogs and even cats, than women. There were a few, but very few; a reflection of how the money was being spent. So far though, it wasn't an issue as we hadn't needed one.

On the face of it then, all good, but the celebratory dinner with Davis and Lawrence seemed anything but. Lawrence was in high spirits and indeed, intent on getting loudly drunk on Louis Roederer Rosé Champagne, however Davis sat under his very own cloud. No matter what I tried, he wouldn't be drawn on what was concerning him. I had no alternative but to let it wait and see if I couldn't work it out at a later date, but I wasn't really drinking either. I wanted to keep my wits about me, as we had Clovis in next day.

'Harry' had died of a drug overdose. Not heroin or anything nefarious, but prescription drugs, though technically, he'd choked on his own vomit. He was an otherwise seemingly healthy 32-year old actor who had made a shedload of money as a teen heartthrob, however his star had faded through his twenties. Clovis had been very particular that he'd wanted someone young, or at least substantially younger than he was. I'd had a concern this might be a difficult thing to find, but infact there were a few quite younger specimens, preserved when their time was cut short, by distraught parents.

Harry had been discovered by the cleaner in the morning, curled up on the floor of the shower, warm water sluicing down on his curled form still wearing pyjama bottoms and slippers, although this information we didn't feel necessary to pass on.

Clovis took no interest in all that was going on around him, no doubt used to being the centre of attention, regarding Davis as one might view a man in to fix the boiler. He was just intent on the ride, impatient for it to begin and quite rude to Davis in the run up. Eventually though, we had him strapped down, coked up, needle in place and all eyes reverted to the screen, as Davis turned on the tap. I was pleased with myself that aside from one minor step, I had remembered the entire sequence, although I also realised that to actually do it was a whole different prospect.

"I was asleep, a cold, hard place, like a sanatorium, I was dreaming of a mouse, a tiny mouse and all it was doing was sitting on its haunches, just twitching its whiskers, looking up, sniffing the air, its little eyes, it was so tiny, was so furry. Then I woke, because I' vomited in my mouth, in my... I could taste.. But I couldn't move.. I wouldn't move.. I couldn't get it out, I started gagging, that stomach-acid burn in my throat I couldn't get up.. and the mouse was gone. It was raining, but I was warm. Nothing made any sense."

What was so remarkable about this debrief though, was what it had done to Clovis. It had stripped away all the bravura, all the pretence, leaving this little boy, a scared little boy. Even his hair look deflated.

The debrief was the best bit, the part I looked forward to the most. Without even planning to beforehand, Davis and I intuitively cleared the room and took the debrief ourselves, uninterrupted, with strict instructions made that we not be disturbed.

But even in his distressed, convalescing mess, Clovis already stated that he was going again. He didn't care what the cost was, he had to do it again, as soon as was medically possible.

Over a glass of wine Davis and I had a second debrief of our own. We had no idea whether it was safe to go again at all, let alone whether there was a specific period of time that needed to elapse.

"The cranium is made up of eight plates of bone..I insert the needle not through bone, but into the brain via one of the sutures, as you know. In theory, it's possible to stick a needle in a different location... minimise the possibility of adverse effects from going in on the same spot, but even so, this is.. new territory."

"But you think it's possible.. to be ok, going again..?"

"Who knows, right? I guess so." He shrugged darkly.

"Look he pays, he signs the waiver, it's all his own risk, right?"

"Tony."

Ok, here it was. I could feel it. This was the conversation I'd wanted to have, but he'd baulked at before. I braced myself. Whatever it was, it wasn't good news.. We'd barely started the whole gambit and already I could feel the cold feet.

"Don't you ever think about, you know, the morality of it?"

"What do you mean?" I knew what he meant.

"Well, what this work has proven, beyond any doubt... we now have what -three different people, including yourself, right, who can testify to the fact that these Neuros ain't dead... They can be woke up. Don't that... say nuthin to you?"

"I guess not enough."

"See, my concern is twofold. As a scientist, as a doctor, I

have a moral obligation to these Neuros, these lives. Every time I do this procedure, I ..I.. I kill that person, you get me?I'm effectively killing that person off. They die a second time, but this time is.. is fatal. I'm like.. Draining the capacitor, you know? Shorting out the little that's left, in the battery. The little that could be.. No, that is the thing to bring them back properly, sometime in the future when someone with more of an idea than me is at the control."

"Davis. But are you learning anything? Each time you do it, can you see a way to extend that.. battery life, or kick the whole thing back into gear?"

"No." His head dropped. "All I'm doing is re-energising, waking up one very tiny aspect of the whole. The rest of it..." He shook his head, brows up, eyes clueless.

So it was the work that was getting him down, the research aspect. The sense that he was failing as a scientist. Some inner part of me breathed a sigh of relief.

"Look, Davis, you can't despair. What is this- the third Neuro you've brought back? Only the third. It's so early doors. We have another... eight here and now, for you to improve on.. Ok, call it seven if you do one yourself, but that's still more than half. Not only that, these things.. they have to take time, right? Look at Thomas Edison."

"I don't have a thousand heads, Tony. That would make me the biggest serial killer in history."

"I know, I know. That was glib, sorry, but the point is, you can't expect perfection, straight off. I think it's amazing what you've achieved already. In such a short space of time. Look at your success rate."

He didn't look very encouraged by my words, but I had a sense that at least by getting it off his chest, he was good for another few. I slapped the table emphatically.

"You're doing great. But this is a human brain, it's not a heart, or a computer even, it's the human brain. That's never going to be easy."

"Right."

No, there was something else. Something he wasn't telling me. I hesitated, wondering whether this was the moment to winkle it out.

"So what do you think about doing the next one yourself.. Who is it... Ian?"

"Ivan... no, I don't think so. Not this time."

"Ivan. By the way, what do you think of 'Peso'? Tony Peso?"

"Sounds good, sounds... American. Is that what you want?"

"I just wanted something more.. Friendly than Pesic."

"What is Pesic?"

"It's a Slav name, my father's side. Antonio was his choice also- the first name of Stradivarius?"

"Strad? The violin guy? Cool."

"Yeah, that's my dad all over. He revered him. I used to spend holidays watching him run around like a wood nymph with a small hammer, tapping on trees."

"Tapping on trees? What for?"

"I never found out."

Davis roared with laughter at this."He never told you? Oh, man. That's tough."

"Yeah and now he's dead."

Davis roared with laugher again.

"So you'll never know!"

"So I'll never know."

"Some secrets die with people."

"I'll drink to that."

We clinked glasses.

21

My happy late-morning coffee musing, in sunglasses under the shade of my veranda, consisted at that moment of posting a rare Facebook update -a photo of the view from my balcony- whilst thinking I'd actually pulled free of Sammie. It was interrupted however, by the sound of a car pulling into the driveway.

Momentary anxiety that I had just conjured the very man from The Depths was temporarily assuaged when I saw Davis emerge with a carrier bag, shortly to plump a newspaper down on the table infront of me. No sensational headline, it was folded back to some terminally dense-looking piece, buried in the geek pages. I looked up at him in hope of a short version.

"Read it."

I steeled myself and made a start. I wasn't a morning person. It was an article charting the spread of a new cyber worm. Cyber worms are malware, designed to take over a computer. They differ from a virus in that they don't need to rely on human interaction to spread, they can do that all by themselves.

It had been discovered by Stanford's research institute in California. There, they were able to monitor how many times it had managed to invade another, unknowing computer, although they were unable to actually do anything about it. The one under discussion stood at over 120,000 conquests at the time of writing and was spreading geometrically.

It being relatively early in the day, it took me three paragraphs before the penny dropped. I looked up at him.

"Is this.. Is this it? Is this.. What I did?"

He didn't say anything, intent on pouring a green tea.

"What are they going to do with it?"

"Whatever they want. With that grab, they can hold anyone to ransom... right now."

"What will they do?"

"They won't wait much longer.. The longer they delay, the more likely it'll get patched. They must have a target in mind, they're just waiting til they've got the power-ratio they want, then they'll hit whoever... a bank... a country..." His smile held no humour.

"Jesus Christ." I stared through to the tiles at the bottom of the sparkling, innocent pool. My dad had died and I'd turned into the most ridiculous Bond villain the world had ever seen. How was it even possible?

"Do we try and stop him?"

Davis looked at me as though I had lost my mind.

"Stupid question. Sorry."

"I know what you mean. It don't feel right sitting doing

nuthin. But you have to ask yourself, what would you do? Who would you tell and would you get away if you did? No. He'd know, you know? He'd know and then you're marked."

"Yeah." He was absolutely right. I didn't know why I'd wasted my breathe saying it, I knew it in my bones. "It's the not knowing though.. Not knowing who he's going to hit... or when."

"Just have to put it out your mind. Tony, I need you to do something for me. I've gotta be back up the lab, need you to make a pick up."

"Sure, what is it?" I said.

"Neuros."

I had no idea why my stomach should lurch at the idea of it. I was already well in, in over my head. But up til now, even though I'd actually done the trip myself, I'd still somehow managed to remove myself from it all. But the idea of actually carrying some heads, albeit entombed in stainless steel, grossed me out. I slugged some coffee.

"I'd go but.. I can't be in two places at once. Pay the guy... Moses... and bring the Neuros to the lab. That ok?"

"Sure. How much is there?"

"$150 thou-."

"Ok. Best I don't lose that then"

He turned to go.

"Take the Benz. I put it in the SatNav.."

"Great. Look, Davis, can't we use the bodies we have, rather than bring in external Neuros?"

This seemed to needle him and he turned back fully to face me before he started, although he stayed calm and measured, like he was explaining to a child something that was obvious to any adult.

"I won't use bodies. Do you understand? There's only maybe 250 cryopreserved people in the whole of America. A fraction of those are Neuros. At our facility, we don't have enough. We have to somehow get them in, ok? And this is how we do that." He shoved the bag with his toe and waited for an answer. He really hated the whole business and my nitpicking really wasn't helping this situation at all.

"Ok, ok. Look, I was just asking. I don't know anything about this, you know that. I'm just cranky in the morning. I don't mean nothing by it. I'll get on it, Davis, right now. I'm sorry."

He nodded, mollified somewhat, but left without saying another word. I looked down at the bag of cash. I'd never seen so much. It looked silly, like play money.

A long drive, the place I needed to get to was over the border in Arizona, which explained why Davis didn't have the time, but once out of LA, the quiet Merc ate up the miles. As I got on the 10 towards Phoenix, the phone rang. It was Sophie.

"Hi, Tony.."

"Sophie?"

"Yes, I just wanted to let you know, I processed your first payment.. Should hit your account in the next coupla hours."

"Ah, ok, that's great. Thanks.." It seemed churlish to ask how much it was: Rude or something, but that was probably entirely the Englander in me. I should probably know that info anyway. Another call nudged my screen.

"Sophie, that's another call.."

"Sure. Have a great day."

I congratulated myself on cutting the connection and not losing Erin on the other line.

"Hey.."

"Hi Tony. You driving?"

"Yeah.."

"Ok I'll keep it short. I just wanted to say hi and whether you wanted to go somewhere, do something. I haven't forgotten you're need of a tour guide. I've been real bad not showing you what a great town LA is."

"Ah, I see. Ok. What do you have in mind?"

"Well, I have a surprise for you later tonight."

I looked at the clock. It was already gone eleven. With American speed limits, this trip was at least four hours there, four hours back. Maybe I'd hit rush hour. Plus I'd be knackered.

"Hon, I can't do this eve. I'm.. I've got this trip I have to do right now. I'm driving out to Phoenix, so I'm never gonna be back in time."

"Ah, ok, no problem. That's cool. It can wait."

"I promise, there's nothing I'd rather do, I just can't today. Is that ok? I'll make it up to you, I promise."

"Ok. So call me when you're back."

"Right. I'll do that."

Ok, Drive safe. Bye."

"Bye."

I looked down at the bag of cash on the chair beside me and shifted it down into the footwell. Life was mad.

American roads were as epic as they always seemed on the telly. Wide, long and straight, with mountains either side in the distance and huge, chrome-wheeled artics forever towing trailers back and forth between cities. I loved America. I needed to work out a way to stay more permanently.

The place I was heading to was the right side of Phoenix and the trip out wasn't too bad, punctuated only by a text from Davis to say there'd been a change of pick up destination and instead of going to the programmed cryonics establishment, I was to make tracks to some random Walmart carpark a couple of miles short of the original target, near Wintersburg. Eventually pulling off the highway, I headed into some pretty barren looking desert, shortly to come across the sign for Wintersburg and then the Walmart depot hove into view. Pulling in and parking up away from the entrance, I took the opportunity to get out and stretch my legs; it was a dry, dusty place that hit you full in the face as soon as you ventured out of the controlled confines of the car. As soon as I did so, my cell went, a number I didn't know. The chap on the other end telling me to look about. I saw a man waving from a little way across the car park. Returning to the car, I drove over, half an eye out for any police cars. Winding down the window, I parked adjacent.

"Tony?"

"Yuh.." How did he know?

"Moses." He didn't offer out a hand, so neither did I. He didn't look much like a Moses either, to be honest. A small, dark, wiry guy I took to being maybe Mexican, but it was hard to know.

"Purple Benz, had to be you. Got the cash?"

"Yeah." Purple Benz. Of course.

"Stick it in there. You mind if I count it? Cans r 'in the trunk. You'll need a hand."

I retrieved the money and slung it via the high pick-up window onto the bench beside him, only latently thinking I should have checked it was all there myself. He sat and riffled it over briefly, whilst I occupied the silence by taking in the desert surrounding me. It was beautiful in its own stark, blasted way, but I could never live out here, so arid, so harsh. The air was hard to breath and you couldn't open your eyes for fear of permanent sun damage. But it was more than that. It was as if, despite man's efforts, nature was so evidently in the ascendant out here. It made us soft, weak, pudgy things that, if we weren't careful, wouldn't last five minutes in this environment. Desiccated, rust-stained dust in the dry shake of a rattler's tail, poet that I was.

With a grunt, Moses chucked it all back in the bag and then did as I had done, shoving it down into the footwell. He then got down and helped me manage the two large cases into the boot of my car, nodded, retreated and drove off.

Ok. That was the harder half of the job negotiated. I'd broken out into a full sweat with all the exertion in the searing heat. Cowboy hats started making a lot of sense, not that I thought for a moment I could ever carry one off. It was a relief to pull the door shut and get the air-con back on. I realised I was thirsty and wondered if I could be arsed to walk over to the Walmart itself, but decided not. I'd need to get some fuel anyway, so figured I'd wait til I found a petrol station down the road. Texting Davis a progress report, I headed out the way I'd come.

By the time I reached the garage, less than ten minutes later, the air con had chilled the sweat on my shirt to the point I was uncomfortable and didn't know how to fix it. I also realised I was starving but, nervous of leaving the car with its precious cargo alone for any time at all, I picked up a ready-made bun with my outsize bottle of water, as I paid and got on my way.

Every time I got into a car and started her up, I'd got into the habit of saying out loud to myself 'drive on the right, drive on the right, drive on the right' three times, like a mantra. And that was ok once I was on a road, but needed thinking about again sometimes at big junctions, where I sometimes worried about which lane to turn into, far happier to be behind another car that was going my way. There were some really wide roads with huge junctions and no clear road markings. But once I was on the right, apart from that sense that the bulk of the car was now on the wrong side of me, needing compensating for when positioning in lanes or when parking, driving stateside was basically ok.

The trip back was fine til I hit the outskirts of LA proper and the traffic began to pile up, til we ground to a standstill. I'd been right to be cautious about agreeing to a night out. It was going to be a late one before I did the drop and got home to a shower and besides, I'd be knackered.

When I arrived at the lab there were a couple of extra cars, signalling activity of some kind. On entering, I was introduced to our newest passenger, a thin, very enthusiastic Chinese businessman called Mr Ding. He was also the first of our clients I really took to. He was very excited and interested in all that was going on and asked a lot of questions before, during and after he was strapped in. He also chatted a fair amount about his own life, although clean cocaine can do that to a person. It turned out he'd come through Lawrence, he was a married father of one and had made his money in plastics. He was also a keen cricket follower, so was delighted to meet someone who actually understood the game, rather than all the Americans he was usually surrounded by.

"We need to do this. We need to start properly investing in cricket. We could be great, greater than India. We already start investing in the sport, like soccer. Start summer schools, get the children educated... excited about it. One, maybe two generation.. Phwwwwt!" He made a flying motion with his hand, to indicate how it would take off in China.

I didn't have a doubt that with such a naturally sports gifted and enormous country, and one that truly understood the meaning of application, they could surely excel at anything, if they put their minds to it.

Ding was duly plugged into 'Ivan'. A Neuro who had, on paper, died of cancer. I couldn't see the interest in wanting to know what that was like particularly, but then we all have our own thing, right? For Ding to be forking out $25million for the privilege, who was I to be telling him what he should or shouldn't be doing with his money?

Davis was subdued. This wasn't unusual, but it was hard to tell whether everything was alright. We really hadn't had a chance to decompress since the testy time we'd had that morning. Certainly when asked, he at least said he was fine; it was always a stressful time going through the procedure to get someone safely linked up, Neuro at optimal temperature, etc. I was just happy to have fulfilled my part and got there in good time, with the requisite Neuros intact. It could wait.

As Davis finally connected Ding, he relaxed a bit and, standing back, finally allowed himself a conversation in low tones.

"Tomorrow, if you don't want, I can debrief.. you driving all day. Tony. I'm sorry if I was pissed at you. It's not you, you know that, right. It's just... you know. It's all stress."

"Hey, don't worry. I'll live. A good night's sleep and I'll be right as rain."

"Right as rain? When is rain ever right? This is California. But seriously, I can handle tomorrow."

"Hey look it's the best part of it. The debrief. It's the bit I always look forward to."

"It is kinda cool, huh."

"Yeah. It really is. You've done something extraordinary here, Davis. It's amazing."

His head went down, but he was pleased. He hit the switch and we both registered Ding's signal, as the trip hit. I felt a need to capitalise on the situation. Be interested.

"Did you do anything different this time? In procedure?"

"I know it can't be the charge. Maybe it's how I apply it.. Maybe I should be lighting up more than just the Working Memory, more evenly throughout, across a much bigger area, you know? Maybe I need to think about the whole thing the other way round. Like.. use the passenger to reawaken the Neuro... seven, maybe eight needles.. That's what I got to thinkin last night. But... there's no time here. I got a job to do. It's not.. There's no room to experiment. Everyone'd get jumpy, you know?"

"Right."

I really wanted to leave Davis and his new army of helpers to see Ding through and get him to the safe house. After my day, all I could think of was a long shower and bed.

"That Neuro was quick to defrost though.."

"They already dropped the temp for me. Impossible to keep it absolute without a constant flow of Nitrogen."

"Am I ok to duck out?"

"Sure. Hey, take that.." He indicated a sports bag on the floor.

"What is it?"

His smile told me all I needed to know. I'd count it when I got home.

Before I headed for the exit, I took a last look at Ding. Twenty Five Million dollars. Who has that kind of cash? I couldn't really picture it.

22

As I drove home, I reflected that with anything, especially an venture like this, there were always going to be bumpy patches. Thankfully, the bumps had occurred over the minor issues and not the major ones. At least so far.

I also figured that whatever Sammie was up to was firstly, none of my business and secondly, too hairy by half to get involved in. What would be would be. And I would just have to carry any associated guilt with my part in that, as and when it happened. How was I to know it was some worm that could take over the world?

As I pulled into my drive, there was a cab sitting outside. The moment I got out, the rear door opened, revealing Erin's legs, looking incredibly sleek, more so by streetlight. I nervously sniffed my armpit. It had that sharp, bitter, nervous stink I was afraid of, different from ordinary, honest, being-hot sweat.

We headed into the apartment by mutual consent, without a word needing to be said. As she shoved the door shut, she reached for me and I had to grab her arms to stop her.

"Please, just let me shower and I'm all yours, but let me shower first."

"Hey. That's my line."

I stood under the jet stream of comforting water, feeling terribly stressed, rather than relieved. America did some things really right and one of those things was showers. Nevertheless, it felt like I was doing a triathlon when I'd only signed up for a swim. Having completed only the ocean component, I still faced a cycle ride and road marathon, before I could lie down and sleep. I'd just about dragged myself out of the surf and it was all about to kick off all over again. Having no friends, no family to properly confide in, or at least totally relax with over a period of weeks, was actually horribly taxing. And I was hardly taking a holiday approach. Something needed to change.

Coming back out fresh-breathed and kissing Erin, I slumped on the sofa harder than I should have and she immediately took hold of my neck muscles and squeezed hard, searching with insistent thumbs.

"Mamad used to get a terribly tight neck. For someone on vacation, you're really bad."

I didn't say anything, happy to resign myself to her handiwork, at least for the time being.

"Did you go to the gym?"

"No, why?"

"Your bag. Looks heavy."

"Were you waiting outside long?"

"I came by earlier but, as you weren't around, I went and

got my toenails done.."

"Does that pass for sightseeing in LA?"

"Depends on the feet!" She laughed.

We kissed long and passionately. As we parted, she looked into my eyes one at a time, carefully. "Honey, are you ok?"

After a bit of a pause and, by way of an answer, I went over, dragging the bag around and unzipped it. The money bulged. She sat motionless, staring for a moment.

"Wow. Don't get me wrong, I've seen a chunk of money like that before... but I wasn't expecting it from you. Where d'you get that? Is it Sammie? You on his payroll?"

Having roughly counted it to the amount of $250K, I got up and poured myself a stiff whiskey, offering one to Erin as I did so. She declined and I sat down beside her and, after a healthy bite of bourbon, just launched in. I told her the whole story, starting with Arif's proposal, then meeting with Sammie. About Davis, the Neuros, not bothered about watching her reaction, as I outlined the basics as I understood them of how a trip worked. And she sat, one leg folded under her, spellbound by the story as it unfolded like a rich tapestry before of her. I worked very hard not to miss anything out. Except.. Except the bit about it being Mamad's Neuro that I had hit. That piece I left out.

And it was a huge relief. I felt -if not cleansed- at least spent. Cathartic is probably the word. And suddenly extremely tired, like I could have just smiled politely as I stood up, negotiated my way to the bed, rested my head on a fluffed pillow and slept the sleep of the giant beneath the mountain. That's how I felt. However, after I'd finished, she had a million questions clambering over each other in their haste to get out. But it couldn't have worked out worse.

I was prepared for her to chuck a total wobbly, shout at

me, throw things, slap me, storm out of the place slamming doors, declaring she never should have let me in in the first place... or all of the above, one after the other. Even the threat of her telling all to Sammie, I was almost prepared for. What I didn't expect was for a little fire to light up in her eyes and the ensuing inquisition, details on details, every step, every nuance about what an actual trip was like. About the various debriefs and what stories had emerged. About whether she was allowed to come to Ding's debrief. Answer: Categorically not.

We did then have sex, but I have to say, even if pressed, I really wouldn't be able to recall enough to be tell you much about it. Sorry Erin.

23

When you have time, time to look back and reflect, you can often drill down to those moments where things changed. When that break point is lost a millimetre over the line, the grip is worn and the pressure just too great, or someone decides, for whatever reason that they just don't like you.

I can't say with clarity when the wheel came off, presumably when I accepted taking the drive across the Atlantic and into Sammie's embrace. But I do remember the moment when something felt really wrong, really really wrong and I should have understood more; known better.

I spent the day with Erin, choosing to go sightsee, in order to defuse too many more questions and she took me to see the Hollywood Walk of Fame. I've seen it on TV; we even had poor imitations in Leicester Square of a couple of film star bronze-set handprints, but the real deal was sleazier and more low-rent than I'd imagined it to be. Hollywood proper wasn't a part of town you'd choose to be in, just somewhere to tick off on the tourist must-sees. There was an awkward sense of shamed intimacy to the congruence of enthusiastic tourists hunting down their particular star of choice, crouching down in the path of day-to-day office workers and misshapen men dressed in poorly-fitting, dirty lycra Marvel comic suits, competing for paid photo opportunities.

Set in their pink 'terrazzo' star, I was struck by how many of the celebrated brass names I didn't know at all. I guess that was excusable for radio, for composers and the like, but filmmakers and actors too... It made me really understand how transient fame could be. Most, if not all of these guys were obviously household names of the twentieth century, but we'd moved on so fast, happy to forget the past. They might even still be alive and in their nineties, but no one cared. All of the squealing foreigners huddled for a photo, were solely owned by the contemporary, the instantly recognisable. And that's how it is. There'd be no floor plaque star for me, but would I be any more or less remembered?

Then on to a variety of shops on Rodeo Drive, where I patiently stood about and made what I hoped were the right noises, but my head was elsewhere. Eventually let off the leash after an early dinner, I made my way on to the safe house. Even so, I was first there and, never having met me, the staff were nervous, so rather than cause a fuss, I got a Starbucks for a Java Chip Frappuccino and waited in my car for the arrival of Davis to quickly smooth things over.

Ding took a good while to come too. I got quite nervous about it, but Davis was solid. Knowing how to be patient, he'd brought one of his papers to read, whilst I alternated between pacing around, sitting by the pool and checking in on the slumbering man every twenty minutes or so. Again,

Davis said I was free to go and do something else, that he would take care of it. Eventually, Ding surfaced. Once the covers were pulled back, various pipes and wires pulled off him, I realised the nurses had plumbed him into some sort of colostomy bag, leaving him free to empty his bladder without mishap. Good idea.

Finally, with Ding sat fully up on his hospital bed, a cup of English tea in hand and a tired smile on his shiny face, we got down to business. But far from the expected tale of morphine hallucinations, or predictably dull views from a rubberised mattress, Ding was full of a desperate urban chase, being pursued down back alleys, his leather soles slipping, not gripping. Thinking of his children, beating on himself for not carrying a handgun. Offering up cell, watch and wallet, but being shot. Not understanding the why, but hating his job. It wasn't a mugging, there was another motive, he was struggling to work out what. The way he described it, it was a raw adrenalin-rush of being the prey, really heightened and then the shock and surprise of being shot, looking down at his own blood leaking way as he lay helpless on the floor. It was also significantly longer than the expected ten seconds. More like thirty, so Ding got a bang for his dime.

What it did do though was leave me really confused. As we listened I didn't say anything, but I did pay attention to Davis and he didn't seem at all surprised that a Neuro that was meant to be an old man expiring from cancer, offered up an LA takedown, shooters, the lot. He asked no confused-type questions that I would have expected, had he not been appraised of what to expect. Come to that, Ding hadn't woken up and said 'What the Hell was that?!' He seemed perfectly at ease with and unsurprised by the denouement. He just enjoyed it and was greatly relieved it was all a trip and not reality. Lastly, that he was looking forward to being reunited with his family.

It wasn't for a good hour before I was able to get Davis fully alone and, rather than serving to cool me down, the additional delay only allowed me to over-rehearse my speech.

"What the fuck was that?"

"There wasn't the time, I meant to tell you. "

"You meant to tell me what? Which bit were you meant to tell me? That Ding made a late change? That Ivan wasn't Ivan, but an extra out of Death Wish..? There was a mix up with the labels? What just went down? How can that happen and I be the only one who doesn't know? What were those Neuros I picked up? Cos that was one that I collected, I saw that. And Ding was booked for a cancer death. I saw that too."

"Originally he was. But he changed his mind and we were stuck for our options. Like I said, it's not like going down the supermarket and picking up some oranges. He wanted something exciting. We had this guy... 'Irwin', so we used him instead. I think it went pretty well." Said Davis.

"Where did we get them from? Why was I buying them in a Walmart carpark? Davis? What's going on here?" I could feel him holding back on me. I knew he wasn't happy doing this in general, but there was something else there. I just didn't know what. It was the first time I really didn't feel like I knew what was going on and I didn't like it. It made me itchy. Made me start feeling like I needed to be looking over my shoulder more than I already was.

"Look, Tony, I don't like this any more than you do. Infact, I like it a lot less than you, ok? But we got another ride to sort out, right now. Ok?"

"What do you mean?"

"Clovis is back for part two."

"Tonight?"

"Fifty.."

"Clovis is staking fifty million dollars for another ride.." I said slowly. Even though I'd planned the thing, it was still hard to take in. It almost didn't make sense.

"Right. And it's scheduled in a coupla hours. So, d'you wanna help, or you wanna take the night off?"

"I'm game."

"Ok then."

That was the end of the conversation. I got out of the way of the cleaners, intent on turning the room around, realising that the nurses were also in the process of putting everything back in place for the next passenger. This was some business we were in.

As I got in the car, my cell went. I would have bet on Erin, but it was Lawrence.

"Mate. That was a humDinger."

"Mr Ding was happy then."

"Oh mate, he was over the frickin' moon about it! A very satisfied customer, let me tell you. He hasn't freakin' stopped. He's already talked to three guys back home about it and is going to talk to another two. Welcome to the big time, boy. Welcome to the big time."

If anything, my early experience of the big time had been a pretty nervy affair, all in all. I can't say I'd really enjoyed it, but then, I hadn't felt that secure in it either. It would be good to just see some money in my own bank, not just the 250K chump change in a bag under the bed, but some real zeroes in my own account. Yes, I reflected, that would make me feel a damn sight better about the whole thing.

"When do you think I'll start seeing some actual real money in my account, do you think?"

"Patience dude, patience. These things take time. It's a pretty big lump we have here, so it takes time to move it about. Don't worry, we aren't gonna kill the golden goose, now are we?"

I laughed appropriately, thanked him and rang off, but as I gunned up the road, it was very clear to me that there was only really one golden goose and it certainly wasn't me. I wasn't even an egg and that made me anything but valuable.

Driving away, I started thinking about the Erin situation. She wanted a trip and I would do all in my power not to let that happen. So many things could go wrong, not just in the procedure, but in her having that kind of proximity to the whole process. How did I know she wasn't playing me, that her allegiances even now, weren't with Sammie? I was pretty sure they weren't. Infact, I really hadn't given a shit if they were when I'd spilled my guts all over the floor last night, or the night before, whenever it was. But she hadn't reacted in a way that made me feel she was at all anything other than invested in us.

Mounting a brow and turning a corner at the same time, I was snapped out of my train of thought by the blare of a startled saloon swerving right at me. I wrenched the wheel, braking hard and swearing as my jaw braced for impact, but we missed each other, more by luck than judgment. Sliding to a halt, I looked in my rear view but they'd already disappeared around the bend, whoever they were. I got a slow-motion snapshot of two faces, aghast, mouths open, travelling too fast on a blind bend. But even as I cursed the driver's stupidity, it dawned on me that it was me who had transgressed. The roads hereabouts were relatively narrow, without lines down the middle and in the immediacy of an emergency, my ingrained English sensibility had taken over. When we'd met on the brow, my immediate instinct was to swerve to the left, but that had been the wrong direction. I'd effectively been driving on the wrong side of the road. I really needed to calm down and focus on what I was doing.

I can't have looked too great by the time I got to the lab and it was Davis's turn to ask if I was ok. Again he offered I take a break and for the first time I clocked that this had become a bit of a habit. Was he merely looking after my best interests, or did he want me out of the way? Maybe I was an annoyance and he preferred to do the science on his own. I decided to keep a better eye on how he was with me. Perhaps I was just being paranoid; I had after all nearly killed three people there, including myself, but nevertheless.

Clovis was after an adrenalin hit this time round, so Davis selected J for John, who'd been out spearfishing and died of blood loss, due to a shark attack. He'd been hauled out of the sea in short order and airlifted by his own medical team, but had died in the air, where they'd then actually started the cryo-process of replacing his blood with preservation fluid. All rather extraordinary really, but then, that was the death of a rich man in LA.

It was only in the debrief a day later, that a dreadful sense of deja vu came over me. Again sat in a chair next to Davis, ready to absorb and wonder at a story to end all stories.. The truth, according to one man at the very end of his life.

"I was running, but it was difficult cos of my ankles.. and my whole foot was coming out the front of my sneaker. I was out of breath, I mean real -not even able to breathe.. I turn round and see this guy coming down on me. Big guy and he's holding a piece and I fall. I fall in the dirt and I'm bawling, begging him telling him he's made a mistake.. 'I got nuthin, I'm nobody, I'm a good man' but he shakes his head jus' once, like I'm wrong and pulls the trigger. Bang bang bang. Three times. Hot slice right through me. I lay back and look up an I see a coupla stars way up in the night sky.."

Looking into his eyes, Clovis was transported. I couldn't break it. We both just waited til the smile died from his face.

"But that wasn't what I ordered... What I asked for. What I ordered was a shark bite. What the hell happened?"

"There was a mix up." Davis immediately looked down at the pad on his knee, as if it might supply some immediate answer.

"You got anything to say?" he turned his glower to me.

"All I can say is I'm really sorry. We both are. I've no idea what happened. But I'm sure we'll get to the bottom of it."

"Yer damn right you will. And you'll give me another trip and you'll give it me for nuthin." He edged his bulk off the bed.

"For that, I bring you an Arab Sheik. Deal?"

"An Arab Sheik.."

"Who'll pay a hunerd mill. So think as both of us paying fifty." With that, he shuffled into the toilet and slammed the door.

I looked at my partner in consternation. Davis shrugged and got up wearily to leave the man to his ablutions.

"You wanna eat?" I ventured. He paused before answering, as if his initial response needed quelling.

"Sure, ok."

Taking separate cars, we rejoined at a small Italian restaurant with wide booths, allowing for some freedom of speech. I didn't need even to start with the questions, the moment we had settled into our seats and given enough to the drinks waiter to be left alone, he started in.

"I needed to get two Neuros in short order, ok, I knew that. They're paying big, right, real big. And we can't let em down, no way. But I got let down... Ok? I got let down. I thought I was getting Neuros from one place, just like we wanted, just as we ordered and then, last minute... There was nothing I could do about that. So I had to go source some somewhere else."

The waiter returned with two rattling tall waters and a bourbon for me. Did I really want to know where they came from? Did I? Two guys iced in the street? What were we now, mafiosi ordering random hits? It was important I didn't stay angry.

"So where are we now? Are we... back on track, or is every trip we offer up from here on the same story, give or take? Is that what we gotta expect from now on?"

"This ain't been easy for me, you know. None of this... none of it.." He tailed off.

I reached out and took his shoulder.

"Ok. It's ok."

Pulling off the mint leaves, he took a long slug of the water, wiping his mouth with the back of his hand.

"As far as I know, far as I can tell, I think we're back on track. We have a more limited menu, but we have a menu."

A new waiter appeared.

"Sorry, we haven't had chance to look, can you give us a moment?" I reached guiltily for the menu.

"Take your time." He disappeared.

"There's something else. You know Erin." It was a rhetorical question. "She called me up. Wants in. Wants a trip." He studied my face as he said this, interested in my reaction.

"What did you say?"

"It's Erin, right? I mean if she wants, she blows it all to shit."

"Did she say it like that?"

"No, no, no. But.. Well, it's complicated right, it's real complicated. We have to do it. One word from her and we're shut down. Am I right?"

"I guess so, I guess we would be, but I don't think she would.. You know, do that."

"Ok, but are you willing to take that risk?" He changed tack. "You put us in a real situation there by telling her.. You get that, right?"

I hadn't really thought of it in those terms, not really, I mean not in terms of what it meant -or what it could mean to Davis. The Golden Goose. That was pretty shortsighted of me.

"Do you have any women Neuros? Does it have to be a woman?"

"Not with us. There's not many at all anywhere in America. But so long as she's not too picky about the trip she takes, then we should be ok. You wanna take up the slack and talk to her about that?"

"Sure, ok. I'm sorry Davis. I wasn't thinking.. I wasn't really thinking, you know, like.. about it in that way."

"It's ok. But we have to be so super-careful now. Now we're doing this, there's a lot hanging on it, right? And then we get The. Fuck. Out. Am I right?"

I raised my glass to that.

"To getting the fuck out."

"Getting the fuck out."

The next time I actually saw Erin, she was in a state of some anxiety.

24

"Hey hon, you ok?" I said, as she came into her apartment.

She'd voicemailed me half an hour or so earlier, asking to meet her at home. Already equipped with keys and the code, I let myself in. I knew from the urgency in her voice, even though she was giving me no details, that it was important. And anyway, with nothing much else to do but educate myself on the finer points of private jets, it was no bother to go round to Brentwood and continue. How the other half lived. With no reason to admittedly, I had no idea about the lives of the rich and famous. But there were so many ways of owning a private or biz jet. One could even go into a timeshare arrangement and then sublet to other fliers. Then there were the aircraft price brackets, from the silly, all the way down to VLJ's or very light jets, which retailed for $2-3million and carried six passengers.

Erin took a fair amount of hugs before she gathered

herself enough to talk.

"Sammie asked me up to the house. I've wanted to go up anyway and spend some time with Laxmi. I've left her alone a bit too much, since Mamad passed."

"Sure."

"So I took her out for a long stretch up in the hills. Really beautiful and quite cool that early. The light was amazing. Anyway, I gave her a good brush and then went in, took a shower. When I got to the kitchen, Sammie was having breakfast and asked me into the office." She adjusted herself on the chair. "It's a funny thing, well I suppose it's not that funny, but Mamad didn't tell Sammie an awful lot about business. He studied hard at college and Mamad never left him short of cash... Proper little playboy he turned out. But in the end, he's still a little boy when it comes to Mamad. He's a bit.. I dunno, in awe of me, though we aren't that different, age-wise. He knew Mamad shared things with me that he didn't tell him. So.. Since Mamad died, a couple of times now he's called me in to sound me out on things.. Or ask me if I know anything about something or other. I surprised myself a couple of times.. Able to help, you know. Thing is, I can't work out if it's a good thing or not. See, it's like he appreciates the help, but he still holds it against me that I was closer to his pop, you know? But look, if I can help, then I'll help. And he knows that. He knows he can trust me. With his dad's stuff at least."

"Right."

"So, Mamad had this running thing with a guy who ripped him off back in the day. Quite a chunk of money, though I don't remember how much. It was when he was still trying to make a go of things. Set him back. And the way they are, that family, they'll hold a grudge."

"Ok."

"So that's when your cyber-worm comes up."

"Not exactly my cyber-worm..."

Yeah, well, He's gonna hit three places, all at the same time. It's mad. Kinda.. brilliant, but really mad. Scary. He's been biding his time, but he's planning to hit this guy who screwed Mamad; some city guy. But he's also going to hit the bank system.. Not a single bank, but the Swift system. You know it?"

"Vaguely." I said, desperately hoping she'd elucidate.

"It's the international method for making transfers between countries. It's separate from the bank itself, it's not the transfer itself, but provides the account details. It's like a massive, non-profit system, all the big banks use it."

"So he can make a bank what.. Divert a transfer?"

"Yeah, I guess. It's huge, whatever it is."

"And what's the third target?"

"It's the Cybercrime Unit."

"The what?"

"The FBI. The Cybercrime Unit. In the FBI."

"Jesus. All at the same time?"

"Yeah. He's still enslaving machines, but those are the targets."

"Why was he telling you?"

"Well, it was like he was really proud of himself. Like, at first he just wanted to tell me he was completing unfinished business, making things right for Mamad, taking down this family enemy, so he could rest in peace. Then, once he started, he just wanted to impress me."

"He didn't want anything?"

"No. I don't think so. He just needed to tell someone. Someone who would appreciate it. No one knows his dad like I did."

"When's all this gonna happen?"

She shook her head.

"Why are you telling me?"

"I had to tell someone. I can't keep something like that to myself. God, I have trouble keeping surprise birthday parties a secret. I would have exploded or something."

"Do you think we should do something about it?" I said, trying not to let too much hang on it.

"I dunno. What do you think?"

I had no idea. The whole thing was mind-boggling. Not to mention the fact that not only was I implicated as the worm mule, it all got seriously complicated when you factored in all that I was up to.

"Do you think he know about us?"

"I don't think so. I've no reason to think he does. He's never... said anything."

"But why did he tell you? He's got no real reason to. Was he testing you, do you think?"

"What do you mean? Sammie's alright. He's not going to hurt me. He just needed to share, I think. He knows I want Mamad happy."

"Sure. I just don't see him taking unnecessary risks, especially with something so big, so important."

"So what are you saying, that my life is in danger now?"

"I dunno. Just thinking out loud, I suppose. Trying to work it out."

"Well, what's to work out?"

"Well, what to do with that information and whether you or I are in any immediate danger, is all."

"I don't see how we can be."

"If he knew about you and me, we would be. At least, I would."

"That may be true." She conceded.

"So how was he? I mean after he told you, what was he like?"

"What do you mean?"

"Well, I mean was he looking at your reaction to it all, seeing how you were taking it. Whether you were onboard at all.."

"Well, I wasn't stupid, if that's what you mean. I did ask him after, why he was telling me.. No, I said, what I actually said was 'thankyou for trusting me'. And he liked that. He really liked that."

"Life's never boring, is it?" I said, kissing her.

"No sir, it ain't that." She said, kissing me back. "So what d'you wanna do?"

"Well, I don't see there's anything we can do really, even if we wanted to, which I don't, especially. I mean, it's not as if he's trying to start World War Three, or wiping out millions of lives. He's just getting some bully beaten up, pulling a bank heist and chucking a smoke screen, isn't he, effectively? That's all he's doing. Just on a deluxe scale. Right?"

"Right." She kissed me again. "Right answer."

25

The next to go was Erin. Two days after 'John', 'Linda' was locked and loaded. It was meant to be Clovis taking 'Kirk' next, but all of us felt, I think himself included, that a short break would be a good idea for rest and recuperation, before he went in for his third. The greedy bastard.

Erin and I had had long chats into the night about the whole experience, the procedure beforehand and the aftermath. We also needed to work out whether we let Davis in on the fact that we were an item, although I had to believe he must know already, or how else would I have spilled the beans to her in the first place?

It was agreed that I be there to hold her hand, like a father at a birth or something. I have to say, I seemed to be more nervous than she was about it. Her line of questions hadn't come from a place of trepidation or angst, more from excited curiosity, of possibility, as though talking about it prolonged the anticipation, thereby enhancing the experience overall.

So there we were. Me leading my coked up lady into the lab, surrounded by a small team of white-coats, to be greeted by Davis. As she got herself comfortable and had her head and body immobilised a limb at a time, it was I that tightened my grip on her hand, not the other way round. And as the needle went in and she closed her eyes in readiness, I suddenly got the weirdest flashback to the moment I met her and that somehow she was going to experience the same moment from her own perspective, which of course she wasn't.

Linda was an accidental death and rather a gruesome one; she fell from an open window, impaled on railings below, which made her brain salvageable, as she didn't actually hit the ground. I had long discussions with both Davis and Erin about the violence of this and whether there might be an alternative choice, but Erin was very happy with it, her argument being 'well, when you die, you die, so it's not going to be a nice thing anyway, is it?' And Davis saying that female Neuros really were very difficult to get hold of, so we were lucky to even have this one. A stark reflection of where the money was.

So that was that and here we were again, Davis and I, dabbling with the Darkest of Dark Arts, in the crypt of a modern-day mausoleum, only this time I was toying with the life of the woman I loved. Did I love her? I looked down at her face, her hair clamped as it was in straps and bits of metal. Yes I did. It seemed like an odd time to acknowledge that. And really not the time to be telling her.

"I love you." I whispered in her ear.

With impeccable timing, Davis pressed the syringe and

there was nothing left to do but study digital dials and lines, watch her face. Make sure she was alright. And there it was.. The hit.

"PoB" I said, to no one in particular.

"What?"

"Oh. It's what they say when you take minicab, back home. PoB. Passenger on Board."

"I like that." Davis said. "PoB. That's cool."

Of course, this time I stayed around, I took a seat in the corner and, when it was time to transfer, I travelled in with her. Finally, I set myself up in a bed in the corner of the now familiar safe house bedroom and pulled out some light reading to be getting on with.

The more I read about Cryonics, the more my respect for Davis grew. What he'd been banging on about in terms of paucity of Neuros also made more sense, in that even though there were roughly 260-270 preserved bodies out there, really it was only the modern-day ones that were going to stand any chance of offering up a trip. The earlier ones, anything before 2001 basically, had been too crudely frozen, allowing ice crystals to expand, destroying all organic matter at a cellular level. The newer the corpse and the quicker it reached the process of preservation, the less deterioration there was going to be. That made absolute sense. These days, preservation, or vitrification consisted about 16 different fluids and antifreezes, taking the patient in need of 'rescue' down to freezing temperature.

Anyone in line to be preserved would be advised to move closer to the cryonics lab or, in the case of millionaires, have a medical team on standby, to fly in and start the procedure, the moment they were declared dead.

Before I'd met Davis and witnessed fully and undeniably

for myself the work he was undertaking, I would have been the first to jump up and declare the notion of bringing someone back from the dead a bloody stupid one, of the highest order. The conceit that we as humans had the march on nature was just for starters. I would then want to discuss the notion that, with any number of poisons pumped into every artery, organ and capillary, how we might then even think we could turn that sledgehammer of chemicals around to reengage a sentient, operational human seemed beyond ridiculous.

But with newfound understanding that bodies continued to digest food, balance hormones, even circulate blood whilst for hours after being declared dead; with these huge strides in the direction of limb and organ regeneration, coupled with the very real knowledge that the brain wasn't entirely dead, even though it had been deemed clinically deceased; these people taking out life insurance policies to cover their cryonics bills might not look quite so dumb. Granted, the early uptakes didn't look too great, those that had gone down between the sixties and Nineties, but as cryo-science progressed..? Who knew?

It didn't bode too well perhaps for those that would become the early risers either, those picked first for resurrection, for there were surely going to be a great many failures before there was to be any lasting success... and God alone knew what pain and torture those early 'successes' would endure- before they really did die. And then there was the mental health side to consider. How traumatic could it be to actually be brought back? How much of the brain would end up being truly functional; sentient? How could it be possible to replace all of those incredibly nasty, manmade, base chemicals with the extraordinary, balanced myriad that powered around ordinarily in ones bloodstream? I mean, If I'd understood anything from my own life experience, watching people get decrepit and die, it was that the drugs we already had in common use seemed to work more by luck than judgment and also that they had any number of unwanted side effects on other aspects of a functioning body. Again for me, it came back to nature: How we thought we would be able to replicate nature to such a degree, well... I wasn't convinced. By which I mean, even with all that I had witnessed in the past few months, I still wasn't convinced I wanted to play lab-rat to future generations of biochemists.

A good few years ago, I was helping my grandmother get into her flat, having celebrated her 95th birthday. She was in a wheelchair, having lost a leg to gangrene, whilst laid up with an unrelated injury. She resided in sheltered accommodation and she liked me to go in first and check that there wasn't anyone hiding in the wardrobe, or under the bed. I also took the opportunity to covertly pick random stuff up off the floor. There might be a carrot under the kitchen table, a few pens and pencils in awkward corners, a knitting needle; the sort of thing that was easy to drop, but impossible to reach from a wheelchair. As I negotiated her in through the door, she said -

"I hope I don't see a hundred."

Of course, my immediate reaction was to remonstrate with such grim talk, but she responded -and I'll never forget- she responded totally lucidly, quietly, having not only thought it through, but having lived it.

"When you get to my age, you are alone. Everyone you know, all your friends, are gone."

And it was true. So she was in a set of sheltered

accommodation, beside neighbours within spitting distance of her own age, but that didn't automatically make them friends. She'd outlived her husband by 25 years. Even her daughter, my mother, had died before her. She, more than anyone, was totally perplexed as to why she had lasted this long and so much longer than everyone else she knew growing up. And the way she said it, the way it was meant, there wasn't any arguing with it. It wasn't morbid depression speaking, just fact, it was what she felt and I totally got it.

No. When I died, I wanted to stay dead.

26

Unlike Ding, Erin seemed to escape from a nightmare. She gave a body jerk, flinging her arm out and emitting a small cry, not at all loud, but not a happy sound. I jumped up and held her, as she opened her eyes and took a moment to focus on where she was, on who was infront of her.

“”It’s ok, everything’s ok. I’m here.”

Through her dishevelled frown, she pushed me off, managing a poor attempt at a reassuring half-smile, before burying her face in her pillow, brought specially.

“Oh Tony. You have to go. You need to get out.”

Davis entered the room.

“Hey..” He said.

“I was just asking Tony to.. let me prettify myself.”

And with that, we were banished downstairs for ten minutes, whilst she saw to it that she was ready for an audience. Far from ideal, because we really wanted that first impression, unsullied by rethinking, but what can you do? We'd set her up in her own place to rest up, partly because she wanted that, but also because it was convenient for us. Clovis had changed his mind and wanted to go again in short order and true to his word, he'd also brought in his mystery Arab.

When we eventually sat down for the debrief she was looking more herself, hair neat, fresh breath, eye make up and even a bit of lippy.

"So when you woke up, you didn't seem too happy.." I said, to kick it all off.

"No. No, I wasn't. I was actually.. It wasn't anything to do with the trip.. Oh my God, the trip!" She said.

"What?" said Davis and I in unison.

"Well it wasn't some awful accident, it was murder. I was.. Linda was pushed. She was pushed off the ledge and... then I fell on the railings. My God it was terrible..."

"Start from the beginning. You want some water?" I rose and got her a glass by the bedside.

"Well, I was sitting on the window ledge and he was coming over as if maybe to kiss me, but as I raised both my legs up, he lunged forward, it all happened so fast.. and he just pushed me, real hard, it was no accident. He just shoved me out the window. I was so surprised.. I saw the look on his face.. this sort of determined.. like sorta angry... the sort of face you want to smack and then I was falling, waving my arms and I said 'Truman' and I was looking up at him and then at the roof.. and then I stopped, real sudden. Jerked my head back and I knew it was bad, but I couldn't feel anything. Like I was floating, it didn't make sense and I felt all woosy, like I should still be falling. And I replayed in my mind's eye what just happened. I recalled I was shuffling to get a good position on the ledge. I wasn't too happy with it, but Truman wanted a photograph of me framed in the window. The late sun was shining through the trees and I could see how nice it would look.. And. And that was it."

"Wow."

"But it wasn't an accident, it was murder. Do you see? We have to do something."

I could almost feel Davis next to me as he slumped mentally, one of those 'Oh God, no. Not this, please not this' moments, but he covered it well, getting up and going over to the imported medical chest.

"We need to find this Truman and make him pay. It's all a game, one big game." She said, squaring to both of us in turn for affirmation.

Davis was fiddling with some medical paraphernalia and, as she carried on winding herself up, calmly administered her a needle.

"Right, right. I see what you mean." I said, wondering what on earth I meant by that.

"You need this, for the... and then you're done. Just rest, get your breath back and we can see about getting you something to eat. What do you want?"

"Huh?" She said.

"To eat. What would you like?" Said Davis, in his best bedside manner.

"Oh.. I don't know. I..." and with that, she passed out.

"I didn't have a choice, man. I mean... solving Linda's murder, right? I mean, Jesus. I warned you this was a bad idea."

"I know. I know. I'm sorry. It was a bad idea, I didn't want it either."

"But why d'you have to tell her? Why tell her anything?" He said.

"She saw the money. In the bag. She saw it. I had to tell her something."

"I mean, what the fuck, man?" Continued Davis, the most outwardly distressed I'd ever seen him.

""I'm sorry. What can I say? What do we do now? How long's she out for?" I said.

"What do you mean, 'how long's she out for'? She's gone, man. She ain't coming back."

I looked at him for a stunned world as his words sunk in, then looked at Erin, at peace on her pillow.

"You took her out? Just.. Just like that..?"

"That's what I'm trying to tell you man, she gave us no choice. She knows.. You know with her, she's not just gonna sit and let that one pass, she's gonna create some almighty stink and people are gonna wanna know how she knows squat -and then.." He made a gesture with both hands like a nuclear bomb going off.

"Jesus fuck." I said, head in hands.

"Look. You get over to the safe house. Clovis is laid up in there. I'll finish up here."

"No. What? What are you gonna do? Bury her in the desert?"

"No need. Calm down, man. Just calm... She signed a waiver, right?"

"Yeah, but.."

"So this is why we pay Lawrence. He transfers the waiver over to a cosmetic surgeon. So it's a 'terrible, unfortunate accident'. 'Medical complications', whatever. He gets paid, we're covered, it's all above board and there's no desert required, ok? She gets taken off down the morgue. Proper burial, I promise. Ok? You get off and I'll sort everything out. Go."

"I loved her, man."

He took me by both arms and shook me gently, trying to engage my eyes, like a father with his distraught son, needing him to see sense.

"I know you did. I know you did Tony, but it can't be helped, right? There was nothing anyone could do about it. At least this way, she gets a proper send off, right?" He clapped me on the shoulder. "Go."

"Ok. Ok, I'm going.."

"K for Kirk. Died of natural causes, old age. Go. Run." He hustled me out of the door.

"Kirk. Ok."

Then calling out to me as I sailed down the stairs.

"And then we got Marco straight after, the next day. So stay on it."

"Ok."

I stumbled out of the house and down the steps, not even sure what had happened had really, actually happened. I hadn't seen that coming. Mind you, I hadn't seen much of what had happened in the last week coming either, to be fair. But Davis was right. What choice was there?

It took me a while to pull myself together and start the engine. I sat in the car for quite some time. It was so hard. Relationships were so hard for me. It was horrendous to think that this thing I'd been building here, after so long in the wilderness, this thing that felt so cool and natural and sexy had just ended and made sense that it had ended. It was all so fucked up. I pressed the ignition, repeating my driving mantra to myself -'drive on the right..'- as I pulled away, watching Erin's house curve out of frame in the rear view mirror, through tears. 'Drive on the right...'

27

My arrival at the safe house was a much smoother affair than previously and I gained entry with a series of subdued, respectful nods and efficient door-openings. It was just as well, as I didn't know what I would have done if anyone had stood up and tried to stop me, being in no mood for polite negotiations.

Sending the staff out, I was relieved to be able to sit in a darkened room with the comatose Clovis and gather my thoughts. Even through those tears, I could see Davis was right. There was very little else to be done. When Erin decided she was going to do something, no one stopped her. I'd liked that about her. But this juggernaut was travelling too fast, with too much invested, the risk too high. I could never have turned her around. As she had said herself, she would have had to have told someone. And who would that someone have been?

But, God. Why me? The safe house was starting to make me feel claustrophobic. I couldn't stand the place. Clovis awoke to the sound of someone dropping something metallic on the marble tiled floor below.

"You can't get the staff these days." He said.

I pulled myself out of my torpor and realised I hadn't got a notepad of any description.

"How are you doing?" I asked.

"Better than you, by the looks of things. Are you ok? Should I get you something?" He countered.

"I'm fine. It's been a long day."

"I can see that."

"Can you tell me, er.. Can you tell me what you saw?"

"Yuh, it was uh.. Well it wasn't what I was expecting but then, when is life ever, right? Or death, come to that."

I managed a weak grin.

"So I was walking through a forest. A real beautiful forest and the floor was covered in.. I dunno what they were. Bluebells maybe. Far as I could see. It was real quiet, sound of birds up in the trees, but I couldn't see them, just narrow tree trunks, light coming down through the leaves and the strong smell of flowers. Real strong. And then I saw this young pig, like a wild pig. He was wagging his tail, rooting around in the flowers, grunting all happy like, I dunno if he was eating them, or something else.. I dunno. And then a voice.. was a long way away, then it got louder, 'Mr Peagrom, Mr Peagrom, can you hear me?' and I opened my eyes and someone was standing over me, in a long skirt, like it was a tree trunk.. And that was it.

"So it was a hallucination? The first bit I mean?"

"Not exactly, I don't think. Just memory. A happy memory I was reliving.. Just before I went. And I was in love!"

"What?"

"Yeah, that was it, that was why everything felt so wonderful. I was 28 and in love, maybe for the first time, I dunno. But it felt so powerful, like it was gonna burst outta my chest."

I leant back in my chair. That sounded a nice way to go.

"You had no pain?"

"Nothing I could feel, no. Just kinda... lost, but lost in a good way, you know?"

"Are you happy this time, Clovis? Are you happy with that? Was that a good one?"

"Hey. Don't get me wrong, the last one was a good one. They' all been good. Why d'ya think I'm back?" He leaned right out of bed, stuffing his evil smelling breath in my face. "What you got boy, you got a genie in a bottle, y'hear me? It's gold. It's better'n gold. It's amazing. Don't let go of it for no amount of money, y'hear me? Not fer no amount. Now, where's that nurse with the fat ass?"

I headed downstairs and through to the kitchen, looking covertly for something that might pass for a fat ass. Unsuccessful, I told the general assembly that he was ready for them and thanked them all for their work, before bursting out in search of the sanctuary of my car. It hadn't occurred to me to replace it. I mean, I could probably have bought or hired just about anything. A Lambo, a Bentley.. even a Veyron, but I'd got used to the purple-mobile. I was so tired.

I'd got addicted to my shower. Having set the temperature just right, I stood under the stream of water for perhaps forty minutes, letting it course over the top of my head, my palms against the tiled wall. Taking one last check of my phone, I set an alarm and sank into bed. No sooner had I done so, the alarm was going off, or so it seemed.

28

I'd slept almost twelve hours solid, but it felt no more than a long blink. My first impulse was to check my phone and to call Erin, if she hadn't left any message for me. I had a full couple of seconds of that, even scrolling for her number, before I realised. And with that realisation came another, just as stark. I had to get out. Even if the wheels hadn't come off yet -and infact they might've.. I had to get out. This was that time. It was all too close to the knuckle, too much bad had happened and real fast. Sammie was about to bring the whole world crashing down and the one thing taping all of it together was me. Well, me and Davis, but he needed to look after himself and he'd proved himself pretty good at that, so far.

Before I left the apartment, I took the time to call through and find out exactly how much was sitting in my own account. It turned out I had just shy of $30million, with another $250K still under the bed. I shifted 25- of that $30million into my Swiss account and then retrieved the sports bag, stuck some extra clothes, my passport and my toiletries on top of the cash and stuck it in the boot of my car. If push came to shove, I didn't need to come back to this apartment. I then went to Avis and hired a Prius, paying the deposit and a week upfront, in cash, explaining that I wanted to hire it then and there, but was happy to leave it and pick it up some point later. I then transferred the bag into the boot of my new Prius. Ok. That was forward planning, perhaps not particularly brilliant, or well-thought through as, for starters, I'd needed to supply my passport, UK Driving Licence details and a credit card, even though I'd paid in cash. But it was the best I could think of for now. I figured it still allowed for a few eventualities.

From there, on to the safe house. I went to call Davis on the way and discovered he'd already left me a message. The Arab was to be known only as 'Sheik M' or just 'M'.. Dangerously similar to the Neuro in my opinion, but no matter. He was indeed passenger for M for Marco, and if Ding had had a humdinging ride, this one was potentially superb; a millionaire sportster, known for his wild ways, who actually died on the job.. Having sex, whilst imbibing every drug under the sun. Unsurprisingly, his heart had exploded. I could see how the Sheik might be keen to sample it.

Ever efficient, Davis had sorted a rotation of crew, so the nurses and security that greeted me were all faces new to me, but at least they too were primed for my arrival. In fact, the security overall was tripled, due to the Sheik bringing his own along with him. It didn't look too out of place here though, this being America and a pretty swanky neighbourhood in America to boot.

Davis was already installed in the kitchen, availing himself a well-earned meal from the chef. He didn't look too great. I nodded my hello's and he nodded back, his mouthful of food allowing him not to have to respond verbally. There really wasn't anything I imagined either of us wanted to say to each other, come to that. I took a cup of fresh coffee and we made our way upstairs.

"If this goes well, there's a lot more. We' got 28 hits on the site.. #Lazarus10 has trended." He seemed oblivious to the many staff lining our route, so I followed suit.

"28? Are you kidding me?"

We entered the shuttered bedroom and he closed the door before continuing, even though two of the Sheiks minions were in there with us.

"No. But three more and I'm done. That was the deal. Do you get me?"

"I hear you." I had to say, I felt exactly the same. Three more, at how much? 50-? 100mill? How much could a guy spend in a lifetime? So there was time maybe for a couple more, before we pulled the plug.

We took up our customary positions. Davis was far better at knowing when a passenger was going to come out of their slumbers, for no sooner had we made ourselves comfortable, but M stretched and yawned, then for a few seconds manoeuvred to check his backside. I wondered if the colostomy arrangement had failed, but when he looked up, he was still smiling. Davis opened a side shutter to give us a little more light, without too much brightness flooding the room.

"M?"

His face lit up and with the aid of his nurse, he pulled himself up as she arranged a bolster of pillows.

Without further ado, the nurses left us, closing the door behind them.

"Please. Call me Emir. You are the men responsible for this?"

"..Yes. Davis, you've already met. I'm Tony. Tony Peso. Pleased to meet you."

"Great men. This.." He shook his head, at a loss for words.

"Emir, may we ask you a few questions?"

"Please." He settled himself in preparation.

"What happened? What can you remember?"

He paused for a moment, weighing his situation up.

"May I speak freely?"

"Please." I said.

"I was lying on my back, on a table I took to be in a kitchen. I was partially dressed, a fulsome woman was on top, riding my manhood. Riding me hard, but I was in such pain. I was in such agonies, writhing, not my manhood, you understand, but she couldn't see.. I was clawing at her flesh.. my breast, my shoulder.. It was like they were being crushed. A spear running through my chest. And then she came on me, my cock was so hard. That's all. I didn't even manage to cum; the pain too great. I just died there, on the table, with something sharp digging in my buttock. I thought a fork maybe. I don't know." He chuckled sadly. "I didn't even cum."

"Any regrets? Concerns?"

"Oh, no listen, gentlemen, please, it was incredible. It was truly incredible. I have never in all my life experienced anything like it. And I have experienced many, many things. And many times someone has not lived up to what they purported to deliver."

I had to say, his English really was impeccable, but then I

reflected, he'd probably schooled somewhere like Harrow, or Cambridge.

"But you. You.. You delivered." He beamed.

Davis got up to leave, understanding that our audience at least for the time being, was over.

"You'll dine with me? The next time I'm here?"

"You're flying out?" I said.

"Yes, alas, I have some things to attend to. A family wedding.."

"Ah that's nice."

"It is, but I come here so seldom now, with everything. It's such a shame. But I had to come and experience this."

"I'll leave my cell number with one of your men.." I said, rising to shake him by the hand.

"Do that, Yes. I must say thankyou."

We exited and made our way downstairs. At the door, pausing to give my number as promised, I then tailed Davis over to his car. He was already seated, engine running.

"Shall we..eat?" I ventured, knowing the answer.

"I gotta get back to the lab. I' call you later.."

There was just something about the way he said it, I didn't like it.

"Sure." I watched him go. It reminded me of when a girl you fancied, one you had managed to persuade onto a first date, was being polite, really didn't like you and couldn't wait to get away. He was saying all the things he knew he needed to, enabling an exit, never to see me again.

I really wasn't sure what to do. I hadn't been invited to the lab and I really didn't want to go home.

So I turned around and went back in, asking the chef for some scrambled eggs which, by the time it reached me, was served up with wild, line-caught, Canadian smoked salmon and a really fine rye bread.

As I tucked in, I reflected for the first time on the life I had left behind. I was unrecognisable from the man who had left London, how long ago? Four months? So much had happened. And, even though I knew my time was up here, I had no yen to return home either. I needed to work on another choice. There was always Hawaii, that forgotten option I had infact started this whole venture with. It still appealed greatly, but it couldn't be a lasting solution, as I was going to have holiday visa issues all over again, soon enough. If I'd married Erin, it would have sorted things out. But that wasn't to be.

Wiping my mouth with the heavy linen napkin, Getting up to go, I was interrupted by the Sheik.

"Tony. You're still here.."

"Yes, I just needed a snack to send me on my way."

"Come, join me. Accompany me to the airport and I will send you wherever you need to go from there. You are the only person I want to talk to. I won't be able to speak of this to anyone who understands. Will you do this for me?"

I figured, for my share of $100million...

"Emir, it's the very least I can do."

"Wonderful. You are a man after my own heart, I think. We shall travel alone, where we can talk freely."

"You're leaving right now?"

"Yes, yes. Unfortunately so. But I have a devoted crew, who will look after me on my flight, you have no need to worry."

"I'm sure you do.."

"Please.."

"I stood up and followed his security to the nearest of the many black Range Rovers littering the drive and indeed the road outside. The one we got into had a solid-looking glass between driver and rear seating, which was finished in the strangest upholstery I'd ever seen. I ran my fingers across it as I slid into the car.

"You are admiring the leather. You have good taste my friend."

"What is it?"

He smiled with pure anticipation for my reaction.

"I don't think you will ever guess. Sperm whale foreskin."

"This is..?"

"It's incredible, no?"

"It's the softest leather I've ever come across."

"I know!"

With that we pulled away and set off in a large convoy to the airport.

"Did you school in England?"

"No, only university, one of my degrees I did at Balliol."

"Your English is better than mine."

"Thankyou. Do you speak languages?"

"No I'm afraid not. We English are very complacent in our thinking, in our schooling. You?"

"I had English, Mandarin, German Spanish and French lessons as a child. It got a bit much, if I'm honest."

"Ah, Emir, languages are never wasted. Is it not said that another language gives a man another soul?"

"You're too kind. Perhaps so. But where are my manners? Would you care for anything, a drink? Cigar? Something else maybe?"

"Just a water would be fine." I said.

He decanted a small, iced bottle of water into a glass and passed it to me.

"Thank you."

"So you are the entrepreneur and Davis the scientist?"

"Yes, I'm afraid so."

"Do not be apologetic, Tony. To be a true entrepreneur is a great thing. Scientists are two a penny."

"You're very kind."

"And you too have been a passenger, I take it?"

"Yes. I was one of the first.. Davis needed a guinea pig, so.."

"A guinea pig. I miss these English colloquialisms." He smiled. "And what was your journey like?"

"It was amazing. Completely different from yours, of course."

"Tell me."

I had to look out of the window as I recounted what I could of my story.

"I died in the arms of the woman I fell in love with." I finished.

"But that's fantastic, right? That's just incredible. What an incredible thing you have here."

A subdued light flashed on the back of the seat infront of Emir and he nodded to the driver in the rear view mirror.

"Please do excuse us, my driver speaks no English."

"Of course.."

His voice came over an intercom, but of course, I couldn't understand a word that was exchanged. Emir turned on the screen infront of him and flicked to CNN, where news was breaking of a massive, overnight cyber attack on Wall Street, as well as the Swift banking system.

"Have you seen this?" he asked.

"Yes. I mean, no.. But it seems serious.."

"North Korea again, you think?"

"I don't know. I think they get blamed for a lot. Them

and the Russians." I said.

"It's true."

"Does it affect you?" I asked.

"No, I don't think so, not directly, but the ramifications have yet to unravel. I've no doubt something negative will transpire eventually. But for now, we're safe. I think."

My hand dropped to my thigh and I felt a hard corner in my trouser pocket. I had to take a moment, not thinking what it could be, then remembered that when I had been booking the hire car, I'd needed to retrieve my passport. I must have then stuck it in my pocket, rather than back in the bag.

"Where is it you're flying to right now?"

"Now? We go straight to Dubai." He was still distracted by the news item.

"I've never been. I'm told it's beautiful."

"Ah, yes, you must come. It's a very modern city, it's remarkable really, how it has changed in a very short space of time."

29

We pulled up at some gates and, after the shortest of pauses, were waved onto the tarmac, to draw up to a very fine looking 747.

"This is your private jet?"

"This I take for long hauls, it has extra fuel tanks, so there's no need to stop anywhere. Would you care to see onboard?"

"I'd love to."

Slipping out of the Range Rover again we were hit by gusting wind and heat on the exposed concrete, shortly to be ushered onto the plane. It was unlike anything I'd seen before, reminiscent of an over-ornate hotel, or how I imagined a super-yacht inside.

"I find it helps to travel in relaxed surrounds, especially long haul." He said, making his way past bathrooms and bedrooms to a spacious seating area, infront of a sizeable, curved cinema screen.

"It's such a shame you don't have your passport. I could take you to see one of the modern wonders of the civilised world."

"As a matter of fact, I do." I said, pulling it out of my pocket like a magician's rabbit.

"But this is meant to be!" He cried, snatching it out of my willing hand. "Give it to me. Give this to the lady."

"This is fantastic."

"But I don't have a thing, no clothes, no toothbrush.."

"Oh, Tony. Please. Take a seat." He turned and had a quiet word with one of the stewards.

"We shall be taking off in no time. How fantastic. It is always better to give, don't you think Mr Peso?Even better than receiving. Allow me my pleasure."

"Well, that's as good a way as any to approach life." I said.

The plane had started moving so gently, I hadn't even noticed, until my eye caught our slow progress through one of the windows. I watched as we passed nested aircraft, flashing apron lights and worked our way out to the runway. In no time at all, we had lifted off American soil and were climbing up to altitude.

"This news today of the cyber attack. It wasn't news to you, Tony?"

I looked at Emir and realised he'd been studying me carefully these past few minutes.

"You can talk freely. Believe me, I understood when I welcomed you aboard that you wanted to come with me. So I took a gamble and said yes. Are you a gambling man, Tony?"

"Well, not long ago, I would probably have had to say

no, but now, now.. I would have to say yes, very much so. I mean, I don't gamble in the classic sense of the word, cards or dice, but I have obviously taken some big decisions to change my life in taking this line of work on."

"You have indeed. And it has paid big dividends, if I may say. But it is over now? For you?"

"Yes. Yes, I think it has run its course."

"And this cyber attack. This was your doing? No, I don't believe it can be."

"No not at all. But I have a feeling I may know the people behind it and.. Well, when it broke, I knew it was the beginning of the end, shall we say."

"It's funny how it can be, when one truly lives by ones wits, one can sense these things, if one is awake to them. If one doesn't get greedy. If one is ready to let go with one hand, in the knowledge that something else will appear for the other, it invariably does."

"I wouldn't have been able to express it so eloquently, but I am indeed walking away, with no idea what will happen next."

"You have no plans?" he said.

"I have a loose plan perhaps to head on to Nepal. I have friends there."

"How many passports do you have?"

"Just my English one. I do have dual nationality, but never bothered to sort out the Swiss passport."

"A shame. Will people be looking for you?" He said.

"I'm really not too sure. As far as I'm aware, things hadn't fallen apart yet. I'm not directly connected at all, but I didn't feel at all safe... I figured it wouldn't be long before..."

"I see."

Again we were gently interrupted by the appearance of a

steward, who then spoke confidentially in Emir's ear.

Emir again switched on the screen, selecting an American channel for my benefit. Almost as soon as he did so, my mugshot was plastered across it. I sat, rooted to the spot, as the newsreader talked with a cybercrime expert about the fact that my fingerprints had been found on a hard drive retrieved by a SWAT team from my apartment, a hard drive with the very worm responsible for the unprecedented attack on the world financial system.

Glancing at Emir, he was entranced too, but as soon as the news moved on to another story, he switched off, only to look at me and burst out laughing.

"Well, Tony Peso. You really are a delight. So many surprises in one day."

"Would it help any if I told you I'm not actually responsible for that attack?"

"I must say, finding the drive in your apartment smacks too much of a convenient denouement. Always, the American baddie these days is the Brit, don't you find? But I must also weigh this against your enthusiasm to get out of the country."

"The way I saw it, I knew the game was up. And I was already a criminal in a foreign country. Somehow, somewhere, it was all going to fall apart and I really didn't want to be there when it did. But I'm as surprised as you are as to the manner of it. I have been very naive, though. Too trusting. I've left myself wide open to this, so I shouldn't be surprised it's happened."

"I have to believe you. I know you are no hardened criminal. I had thorough checks run on both you and Davis when this adventure of yours first came to light. I had to. So I know all about your schooling, your father passing away, even your Home Office SIA licence. The worst you have against you is six points on your driving licence."

"So. What will happen when we get to Dubai?"

"What do you want to happen?"

"I don't know. I need to get far away somewhere, where I can't be recognised. Perhaps I need a new passport. A new ID. I hadn't really got beyond getting on a 747 that was leaving the country.. I hadn't figured I'd be fingered for something I didn't do. I just worked out that the thing with Davis was probably at the end of its run."

"You have a style and panache that leaves most Brits in the dust, my friend. Would you care to eat? My chef can rustle up anything you'd care for.."

"I'm not sure I'm hungry."

"But I'm also of the opinion that if he put something under your nose, you could be persuaded to eat. We shall see."

Almost immediately, two starters arrived and I found myself tucking into a very fine, cold carpaccio.

"The unfortunate thing, whether you did this heist or not, is your passport really won't be welcome almost anywhere you land in the civilised world." He said.

"Agreed."

"I wouldn't be able to smuggle you off at Dubai, however much my heart wants me to. Everyone will know you are on this plane."

"Agreed also."

"However, I am prepared to fly you on somewhere... however, the other unfortunate thing is, although Nepal might be a wonderful place to fly on to, it's one of the only international airports that simply isn't big enough to take a 747. No large aircraft can land there, due to the runway being surrounded by such high mountains."

"I see." My heart sank again. I hadn't thought of that.

"I think, what we need to do is come up with a plan in the next few hours. What I can also do is organise a midair refuel once we've emptied the tanks somewhat, so that we can touch down and you can turn around and take off again immediately."

He really was taking my predicament very seriously, considering we barely knew each other and I had since appeared on Interpol's Most Wanted list. I was really humbled by this man. Who else would go to such lengths, at such cost and at such great risk to his own personal freedoms?

"Emir, I really can't thank you enough for all of this. But it's too much. You really are well within your rights to simply land somewhere and hand me over to the authorities there."

"Nonsense. Where is the honour in that? I won't hear of it. "

The carpaccio was followed by three more courses, but I was surprised by their familiarity. Rather than the ridiculously exotic I had expected, we had bangers and mash, with heavenly gravy and a jam roly-poly to finish. There was a cheese platter on offer, but I really couldn't squeeze another thing in.

"Have you any idea where else you'd like to go?" he said?

"I think heading home, I mean to England, would be too expected of me. I can't think of anywhere I could go there where I'm not known. My face must have been plastered all over the UK press, as it has been in the states."

"Yes, of course. I tell you something we may be able to do.. Do you have a passport photo on you? I mean other than the one in your passport? We need a fresh one."

"No. I don't think so."

"Right." He said. "Follow me."

The moment he chose to move, it was as if the entire aircraft moved with him, staff stood to attention at every turn, followed every move, but never in the way. All of them with the single-minded purpose of ascertaining his will, in order to make it come true. It was amazing to see, to be a part of, if only as his guest.

When he found the room he wanted, he spoke rapidly, quietly, with authority, but not in any sense in an overbearing way. The path suddenly cleared for me and everyone looked at me, as a large leather-bound swivelling chair was indicated, by a woman holding something similar to a barber's apron. Taking my cue, I was suitably wrapped up and turned to face the strongly lit mirror. Emir pronounced again in Arabic and the process started.

"I shall leave you in their capable hands. But never fear, I shall be back shortly." He said.

My hair was first washed and then dyed a much darker hue. My face was then massaged and shaved, but shaved to leave the faintest of goatees. This beard was then painstakingly augmented with what appeared to be real hair, by someone who must have trained as a movie make-up technician. I was then tanned with make-up and my hairline and style altered.

I didn't look recognisable, even to myself.

"You see?" Beamed my host, over my shoulder. "Now come."

I was presented with a complete change of clothes, two suits and some more casual wear. I dressed, careful not to get any make up on my collar. We then went round the corner, where a digital camera and lights were set up. Here, my photographer took fourteen snaps before he and Emir were happy with one of them. Emir remained delighted with the whole circus of it. It certainly used up the time. Finally and I say that as though it was a long time, but understand from start to finish must only have taken three hours, I was presented with what to all intents and purposes appeared to be a Swiss passport. I opened it up at the picture page to see a man who looked just like me, but nothing at all like Tony Peso. It was brilliant. We were both in hysterics at the brilliance of it, pointing at the picture and then at my face, crying with laughter, like eight year old boys. It was like I'd known this man all my life.

"Tony, my friend, I think we have the beginnings of a plan. Do you have any more thoughts on where you should like to go?"

"Well, I think I need to go where I don't stick out like a sore thumb. I thought of Australia, but I.. I don't know anyone there."

"Nowhere in Europe?"

"What about Scandinavia?"

"Not very warm, but if you like. What about Spain..?" He said.

Before I could respond, a small bong announced that we were commencing our descent into Dubai. We strapped in, smiling across at each other periodically at the absolute gas we'd had, messing about with my face. I couldn't remember the last time I'd had such a good laugh.

"We haven't refuelled. It would make the plane too heavy for an easy landing. They'll wait til you've taken off again and do so up there. Spain?"

"Ok, Spain it is." I said.

Upon landing, as we taxied, there were more complications, which Emir dealt with calmly and efficiently. He bade his farewells there, knowing that the plane was literally going to drop him, turn tail and fly straight back out again.

"What we've also done is change the flight ID. What that means is, this aircraft is no longer this aircraft, but an entirely different one, so wherever you land, they won't know who is on board."

"That's genius."

"It's a little trick we use sometimes, when we need to."

"Emir.."

"You have no need. No need to thank me. You have given me the trip of a lifetime and I hope I have given in kind."

"It has been the funniest time I can remember in a long time. I hope we can see each other again some time."

"Yes, that would be wonderful." He said. I hoped he meant it.

The door unlocked and, with a blast of hot air from the desert and a last, warm shake of his hand, he was gone, the door closed again. I really wanted to follow him. To stay within the halo he cast by his mere presence. It was a charmed and dangerously alluring place to be. Peeking through the window revealed a massive armada of cars, many of them police, some of them possibly army. I had no idea whether they were there for him or me, with him, or against.

I retook my seat and looked out of the porthole, as a stewardess served me a tall glass of water with a rind of cucumber in it. Beside it, she laid my UK passport. I tapped the one through my pocket and grinned all over again. What an amazing man and what a truly unique experience.

30

The aircraft wheeled around and made it's way out to the runway. In no time we were again banking sharply, climbing into the sky. I'd completely lost track of time. Even what day it was. But how was I going to manage in Spain? I knew no one there and I had a real concern that I wouldn't be able to access any of my money, from either my UK, offshore, or Swiss accounts, on account of my name.

A steward appeared and I smiled at his approach.

"His Highness wanted to present you this." He said. With that, he deposited an elegant Samsonite shoulder-bag and backed away. I opened it to reveal a complete, bespoke toilet bag, some leather loafers, two silk shirts, underwear, a mobile, sunglasses, a notepad and pens, two fat packets of US dollars and another of large denomination Euros. It felt rude to count it. God, that man had style.

An hour or so later, not one, but three stewards

approached. Between them, they handed me a headset, turned on the screen and then departed, as Emir appeared on it, larger than life.

"Emir.."

"Tony. I trust everything is ok? They are treating you well? You must feel free to take a bath, or shower. Just ask, anything you want. There's a bedroom also waiting for you. You mustn't feel you are only to use that one chair.."

"Emir, how can begin to thank you for all this.. And".. I held up the shoulder bag.

He waved his hand as if it was already forgotten.

"Tony, I have some bad news, but I hope already to have an answer of sorts."

"Ok, What's the bad news?"

"The bad news is that we, that is my government, have come under significant pressure to deliver you back to the United States. So it pains me, more than I can tell you, but we have had to comply and redirect your flight to Los Angeles."

"I see. Emir, that's ok, really... I couldn't ask anything more of you."

"However, what I have asked the pilot to do is to divert, as late as he is able and land somewhere nearby, maybe Phoenix, Tucson, Vegas, San Diego.. I don't know. And there is still time and there is still a plan in place, but I'll let Shez explain everything to you. I'm really sorry. I tried everything. But the point is, you should have time to disembark before the authorities get to the airport, whichever airport that may be and there will also still be confusion as to the identity of your flight, am I clear?"

"Yes, I see."

"So just follow Shez and she will explain everything for

you. Ok? And give her your passport and she will get an American entry visa made up for you."

"Right, ok and thankyou again, Emir."

With a smile and a slight bow of the head, the connection was severed. I took off my headset and turned to see a stewardess waiting.

"Shez?"

"Would you care to come with me, sir?"

As we walked she started explaining the plan. Unlike a standard passenger jet this one accessed all areas without hindrance. We walked through and then down some narrow stairs to find ourselves in a compartment with aluminium containers, presumably the sort used for luggage, but in this case it appeared to be from the kitchens. Opening one such container, it had been refurbished with a firm mattress and quite a few comfy cushions. There was also a bottle of water and a torch.

"You will be fine in here, the container will be unloaded through the cargo bay, it will be put in a train and towed across to the baggage terminal. Unfortunately, we won't know anyone there, because we aren't yet informed of which airport we will be landing at. The pilot will most likely leave it as late as he can and then request an emergency landing at any offered airport in the area. So, what you will need to do is look out through here.." She indicated a previously unseen line of holes at eye level and a cunning catch and door, which would allow me to slip out without having to clamber out of the top of the container.

"His plan will be to land at as small an airport as he can find, to maximise your chances, with the low number of staff. We will also put one of our men on the baggage train to assist you, airside. What we are hoping is that we can get you on the ground and holed up, perhaps in this container, until you are able to get out and mingle with passengers from another flight, then exit with them through the terminal, rather than attempt to avoid patrols, or climb fences..."

"Ok, that sounds like a plan, thank you."

"I shall come and find you in good time and get you comfortable in here, Mr Danzig."

Tony Danzig, yes, my new name. I needed to get well acquainted with my new details, name, date of birth, where the passport was registered, etc. I thanked her and we made our way back up to the passenger deck.

I started to memorise the details in my passport before passing it to a steward and, as Emir advised, took a shower and then retired to the biggest bed I had ever seen. I slept until I was woken by Shez, who very apologetically informed me that it was an hour before our descent time and that I needed to get back into make-up. I clutched at my face. I'd entirely forgotten that I needed a new beard put on and some tan. Rinsing my face, I got into the lighter of the two suits and made my way to make-up, which was a quicker job than the first time, as presumably, everyone knew what they were doing. Newly made up, I retook my seat for landing and, as soon as we were trundling towards the buildings, I was escorted back through the plane, via a host of smiling goodbyes, to the cargo bay.

"We've landed in Burbank."

"But that's LA, that's fantastic."

"We're very pleased, yes, it's a smaller airport and hopefully not too far from where you wanted to be."

"Do thank the pilot for me." I said, climbing in.

"Take this kit also and put them on as late as you possibly

can. Fingerprints. I'm told they're very simple to apply. The glue is included." She handed me a small kit with Chinese writing on it. "Goodbye Mr. Danzig. Safe trip."

"Thankyou, Shez." With that, she passed in my shoulder bag, now swollen with the second suit and closed the lid. Shortly thereafter, I felt us grind to a halt and the hydraulics wind into action, opening the cargo bay. My bin was shoved onto a conveyor and out of the aircraft belly and then onto a wheeled rack, with much clanking and scraping, as I was presumably joined by other containers. As we snaked away, we passed a couple of police cars, making their way to the aeroplane. The baggage train slowed to a halt and there was a few minutes pause. Then it took off again, only to slow and stop again.

"Mr Danzig..."

I needed no other encouragement, slipping the bolt, I opened the side door a fraction and it was pulled up quickly from the other side.

"Come with.." Said the man.

I shouldered my bag. Looking both ways, I could see we'd swung into a baggage area and the way the train was parked, it hid us from view. Closing the door quietly behind me, we slipped between containers and found a corner.

"Wait."

He disappeared and I caught my breath. It was just unreal to think I was in the Middle East half a day ago, having been in America half a day before that. But it was a good ruse to come back here, hopefully the last place they would think of looking, once they discovered I wasn't on the flight they thought I was on. Hopefully, they'd be looking everywhere else but LA. I just needed to hole up somewhere until I could grow my beard out a bit better and then think about a more long-term plan. I hadn't forgotten my Prius hire car. The complication there being I wouldn't be able to walk in and use it. I just needed to get into the trunk and retrieve my bag. I had the keys. I had no idea how much cash Emir had left me, but another quarter mill wouldn't go amiss. My musings were interrupted by my returning aide.

"Next big plane, eleven minutes only. We wait, then... Ok?"

Ok." Ten minutes wasn't gonna hurt.

"You these.." He passed me some grey overalls. "So. I in building, ok? Then in toilet.. Take off...." He mimed dressing, undressing.

"Take off the overalls, right."

"Right. When people come, you.. ok?"

"When they come past, I mingle. Got it."

"Ok." He grinned. He placed my shoulder bag in a bin liner and handed me a prop bucket. After another recce, he beckoned me out and we shuffled, head down, out of the building and across an airport roadway to the large building on the other side, passing airside workers, going about their business. We passed few more doors and then entered a covered walkway. I could see at the end was a locked door, presumably requiring a pass or code of some sort and I could feel the concern in me rise with every step, as I stayed with him, clutching my bucket. He started talking to me, conversationally, in a foreign tongue, to this day, I have no idea what it was, but it calmed me and I just reacted to the intonations with what I took to be appropriate noises, agreeing, smiling, whatever. Sure enough, we passed some men I didn't know were there, to the left. When we reached the door, his conversation got more animated and he slowed to a stop and then started laughing uncontrollably. I stood looking at him, not sure whether to join in. As it was, he was making such a spectacle of himself, that is was funny to watch anyway, so it made me smile genuinely. The door snapped open as someone breached it from the other side, but my man didn't make an immediate reach for it, only stepped towards it with no hurry, turning back to me, basically forcing the other guy to stop and hold it ajar. With perfect timing, he recovered enough to accept, waving his apology as he did so.

"Must have been a good one.." He observed.

"It's the way I tell 'em." I countered.. and we were in.

We walked until we found a public toilet along a long, plain, deserted corridor and made our way in. Ascertaining there was nobody there either, I was quickly out of my overalls and straightened up. He pulled out my briefcase, then stuffed the overalls in the bin liner, which he then stuck in the bucket. The pair of us looked at each other and, having passed muster, grinned and shook hands.

"Good luck." He said.

"Thankyou. What is your name? Your name..?"

But he just smiled and waved a small wave, then he was gone. I watched the door close behind him for a moment, then made use of the loo. I then spent some time checking my appearance in the mirror and repeating my name, my date of birth and the place the passport was issued, deciding as I did so to give myself a slight French accent as I retrieved my new fingerprints and pulled open the pack. I soon got too Inspector Clouseau with it all and scaring myself silly. Anyway, what would I do if anyone then decided to speak French back to me? The sound of footsteps in the hall, then voices. I waited, locked in a cubicle, until I was certain it was a full flight and not just a small party, then took a couple of steadying breaths and headed out.

As I walked, I realised I had no idea where the flight had come from. My problem evaporated however as we rounded the last corner and a big arrivals board signalled we'd come in from Dallas. Looking around at my fellow passengers, it seemed to fit. I joined the queue of aliens, of which there was only a handful, it being an internal flight. I then had a small panic as I remembered I'd given my passport back to Shez. I squished my pockets, but they were empty. I went to the shoulder bag and again drew a blank, as I was forced to make my way to the waiting Homeland Security officer. His hand out, he said -

"Where did you start your flight, sir?"

"Dallas." I said. All I could see in the bag, all I was staring at, was my old, genuine British passport. It appeared to be glowing, willing me to take it out and hand it over.

"Is everything ok, sir?"

"Yes, I just.."

I scrabbled around in the bottom of the case, my arm constricted by the massive packs of cash crammed in there and aware I needed to be really careful with my fake fingerprints.

"I mean, where did you enter the United States, sir?"

Damn it. I'd got so close.

"Sir..?"

In resignation, I pulled my hand out and as I did so, caught sight of a smaller, unnoticed second side-pocket and unzipped that. Where of course, it was. With a tidal immensity of relief, I pulled the booklet out and opened it as if to assist the officer, knowing I desperately needed to see for myself where I was meant to have entered the country. New York.

I passed over the document.

"New York. I've been travelling around the place. Michigan, then down to Kansas City and then Dallas."

"You flew there?"

"No, no I took the train and drove some." I said.

"Place your hand on there for me, sir." I did so and he went silent as he ran his checks.

"Ok. How long are you planning on staying?"

""Oh, a couple more weeks round California, then I have to get back to work."

"What is it you do?"

"Accounting."

"You don't have any plans on living here?"

"No. I live in Switzerland."

"Have a nice day, sir." He stamped the passport and waved me on. I had just sweated bullets. It was more nerve-wracking than being strapped into Davis' contraption. But I was in. I wondered what had happened to him.

31

From Burbank, a cab ride to the Avis compound. It was difficult to get my head around the idea that I could just walk about freely; my appearance so different that even if someone had watched the news and then looked at my face, it would be highly unlikely that they would twig it was the same guy. As unsuspiciously as I could, I made my way through the serried ranks of dormant cars to mine. It looked ok. Hand shaking, I popped the trunk and there was my bag. Lifting it out, I locked the car and left the keys on the windscreen wiper, then thought better of that idea and took them. They'd have spares and there was really absolutely no point in advertising the fact that I was back.

So, what now? As with carhire, the trouble with hotels was they'd want a credit card, even if I intended to pay in cash. I'd need to go to a pretty seedy part of town to find anywhere that would take cash without asking for further surety. Then I remembered Erin's house: Presumably, that would still be empty. It would be a while before anyone started to sort that lot out? It gave me a few days, surely. I headed out of the compound and bagged another cab. I got him to drop me a block away and made the rest of the way on foot, even though it was hard going with the two bags. Making a couple of passes, all looked ok.

I let myself in and disabled the alarm, then checked the whole place thoroughly, apart from her bedroom. I couldn't face going in there, let alone sleeping in that bed. I made the sofa comfortable, washed and scraped the crapola off my face and gratefully took to my slumbers. These days sleep seemed to be my only respite.

An earsplitting racket directly adjacent murdered my sleep and after a few manic moments bolt upright, getting my bearings, I worked out it wasn't the FBI blowing the wall in, but the gardener using a leaf blower just outside the window. God. This 'being on the lam' malarkey was no good for the ticker. Having demolished a large carton of Coconut water and a piece of dry bread, re-appetised into toast, I sat down with my two bags open before me and worked out what I had and what I needed. I couldn't stay here. It was just guesswork as to when someone was going to come round wanting to start something.. Clearing up, going through papers or the like. She might even have cleaners with keys, I had no idea. I couldn't afford to be found here though, or even seen by anyone.

When I totted up, I had just shy of 350K in US dollars and 80K in Euros. It was a tidy sum, but it wouldn't last indefinitely. I probably needed to buy a car, a decent one that wouldn't die on me. Which reminded me. I turned on the TV and struggled for a news channel. My anxiety dropped as first a story of a Police shooting and then a plane landing sideways in high winds seemed to dominate.

"...At the top of the hour then and our main story: Tony Peso, AKA Anthony Pesic, a British national, now America's Most Wanted, not only in connection with the recent cybercrime that netted him several billion off the international banking system Swift, the taking down of a top-100 Nasdaq-listed company and the attempted blocking of the FBI, in an effort to hide his tracks, he is now also wanted for two murders. Over to Kim, in Wintersburg, Arizona. Hi, Kim, what can you tell us?"

"Ah, hi Shelley, yes, I'm here in the little town of Wintersburg, West of Phoenix, Arizona. And it's just here, in the carpark of a local Walmart that Tony Peso was filmed by this man, Moses Brown, now turned State witness, paying for and picking up two severed heads. I kid you not. Two severed heads. They were hidden in two large cases, but you can see here footage of Tony -and clearly it is him- putting the money in the driver's seat there.. And here again, taking two frozen heads out of the back of the pick up. Here we also have additional Walmart footage as he leaves the carpark -and again here, he's calmly filling the car at the gas station just down the road there and buying himself a roll. This is quite clearly a man exhibiting no fear, no remorse, no guilt for what he's done. He's a man involved with some of the biggest single crimes that this country has ever witnessed. And these two gruesome deaths, well, they were two guys going about their business, late at night in Phoenix. Their names have not ben disclosed yet, but I can tell you from eye witness reports, that one was returning to his car, after an evening out with friends and the other, a down-and-out who may have been picked on, simply because he was vulnerable. Both of these men were shot, several times. Now. Let me make clear, there's no indication at this moment that Tony committed these murders himself, that looks to be extremely unlikely. He did however potentially order them to be done and paid for them -as we have seen, personally, in cash. 150 thousand dollars. Now, that's a lot of money. Why did he pay so much? Well, by the time he received them, the heads had been removed from their bodies, where, we aren't yet sure. These heads were then cryogenically frozen, that is to say, they were frozen very carefully, for preservation purposes. So, still a lot is unclear at this time about one of the most bizarre and unpleasant crimes in living memory. This is Kim Devereaux, outside Wintersburg, Arizona, passing you back to Shelley in the studio.. Shelley."

"Kim, thankyou very much for that. Now, I have with me here in the studio Dr Simon Bergen, a well-respected scientist and expert in 'Cryonics', is that right?"

Yes, Cryonics, the science of freezing.. Of preserving bodies after they are declared clinically dead, with the intention of 'rescuing' them, or rebooting them if you like, at some point in the future."

"Ok, Thankyou Simon and thankyou for taking the time to come into the studio to discuss this with us. Now, my question is, why would Tony Peso, or anyone, come to that, why would they want to purchase frozen, severed heads? Why would he do that?"

"Well, we aren't actually fully sure of the answer to that yet.. But he may of course have been conducting experiments on them and needed specimens.. We're helping the police right now in tracking down where he might have done this, because, as you can imagine, there aren't that many places where large quantities of liquid nitrogen can be easily or safely stored, so the police investigating universities, research labs and of course, cryonics establishments in the area."

"Thankyou Simon. Well, there you have it, the story so far. But what's really remarkable about this is the breadth of this man's criminal capability.. From cyber crime on a massive scale, to mafia-type hits, to one of the darker areas of science with the freezing -or unfreezing- of dead bodies... now, some are already saying that they don't believe it. They don't believe that in such a short space of time, that one man can be capable of committing all these various crimes, but also that he could be expert enough in all of these very different, ah.. specialties. So we're now going over to.."

Switching off, I sat in shock for a long while. Was I really that man? I wondered what my mum would have made of all this. Without doubt, this news had reached England and the living room of my uncle. It was presumably impossible for me to go online at all, check emails, Facebook, not that I ever did. But I needed to consider all of those things verboten. There was nothing quite like a fresh perspective. All of the events had indeed happened and I'd been involved in all of them, but Criminal Mastermind, I was not. Returning to the fridge, I scanned the shelves for anything I might have missed. Erin was never one for cooking and the wide shelves were full of fruit and veg well beyond any attractive phase, Almond milk and a pack of low-fat yoghurts. Well, it was better than nothing. Unfortunately, it wasn't enough to keep me away from switching on the TV again.

"...Obvious proof being the fact that the hard drive in question was purchased in the UK and brought over here, but that could be anyone and again, we're only taking the police word for that... we have been told that Peso's fingerprints are on the casing.. ok, but how would such a highly intelligent individual be leaving his dabs on such incriminating evidence, then leave it lying around his apartment? Something doesn't fit right...maybe he did one of these things and he's the fall guy for every other crime the FBI can't solve."

"Well, thankyou Roland for an alternative point of view. One counter-argument supported by fact, is that he left his apartment, if not the country, in a hurry. So perhaps he didn't have time to cover his tracks as well as he would have liked..."

If it was nuts now, how would it be when they found out about Emir and my private super-liner flights in and out of Dubai? This thought afforded only a temporary smile. What was I going to do? Where would I go? Who would welcome me now? No erstwhile friends. Even if I made it back to Dubai, my newest friend Emir couldn't help me any more than he already had.

"...Now remember, if you see this man, do not approach him. Dial 911, call the police..."

I sank to the rug and contemplated my wretched self. What had I been doing all this time? I'd been in some sort of bubble. Infact, it felt like I'd been in a bubble all my life and time had just been passing by. When my father died, I'd just exchanged one bubble for another, but it had been just as removed from reality as the previous one. Nothing I'd done held any intrinsic value, any worth in the true meaning of the word, however many millions it had made everyone. I wouldn't be able to attend Erin's funeral, I wouldn't even be informed when it was, let alone be invited. What had all of this been about? Really?

I stood up and wandered through to the mirror hanging in the entrance hall.

"What were you trying to do?" I asked. "Was it just about money? What were you planning to spend all of the money on?" I stared back at myself, waiting for a response. I wasn't even sure what I was going to spend the 400-odd thousand dollars I had lying on the floor in the living room. It had all felt so real, I had felt alive, right on the edge of things, as though I had purpose and what we were doing was extraordinary, but in a good way. How had I been so wrong, so consistently blind to it?

How did one drop out in a country? For some reason the idea of it in England seemed clearer, if harder being so much smaller. Being a foreigner abroad made it all so much harder to melt into the fabric. Just absconding, maybe burning my documents, taking a false name and trying to get casual labour, hopping across the country, washing dishes, washing cars, fruit picking? agricultural work? Without a Social Security number the work prospects had to be limited. Nor did I know enough to last five minutes in a casino. I couldn't safely tap my own money, I doubted I could open a new bank account without a home address and a lot of answers I wouldn't be able to manufacture.

I'd been holding off, but there seemed less and less point. The bourbon had been staring at me throughout my TV massacre and now its silence had turned Edvard Munch. With the first measure of certainty I'd felt all day, I wrung its neck and sploshed myself a hatful. Tomorrow would present itself soon enough, but right now, what else was there to do, but self-medicate to absolute quietness? I raised my glass.

"America's Most Wanted. I am the resurrection, and the life: he that believeth in me, though he were dead, yet shall he live: And whosoever liveth and believeth in me shall never die."

Hadn't Munch had something to say about that? I lumbered around my addling mind, groping in dark caverns for a discarded education.. Something.. Scandinavian about flowers growing from his rotting body.. I'll drink to that.. "skol."

32

It must have been three or four in the morning when I was woken in time to see a bag go over my head. I didn't scream, I didn't fight; I figured it was coming to me. I was just unsure whether it was CIA, the Police or the FBI. Someone was gonna get a Gold Star. I was already dressed, for a while kidding myself I was so in the vain hope that, should I hear anything, I could make a quick exit, but the truth was I had passed out as I was, on the sofa. Maybe they were good, or I slept too soundly. Either way, I was cuffed and banged to rights, being walked outside, between what I took to be two men, my head shoved down to avoid smacking the roof of the car as I negotiated the back seat. No one spoke to me, nor did I venture anything. I figured, whatever I needed to know next, I'd be told.

After a swervy drive that did nothing for my head, we slowed to a standstill and the door opened. I was pulled out, walked a short way and then in through a solid sounding door, a corridor another door, and then another one. It was funny being blindfold. What your mind clung to in it's search for clues. Eventually to be sat, wrists still manacled, before the bag was finally removed. Sitting under it, even in the cooled car had made me sweat profusely and my hair had matted to my soaking face. Through out it all I had felt calm, resigned to the inevitability of the situation I now found myself in, my only question mark being 'who?' But, far from finding myself in a precinct, cell, or interrogation room, I was in very familiar surrounds.

"Davis.."

So it was Sammie all along. Had he ordered Erin? Davis didn't say anything. He was busy readying a Neuro.

"You gonna snort this, or do I have to inject it?"

I looked at the coke.

"I'll take it, s'ok."

I leant forward awkwardly over the tray and snorted the coke, coughing and wheezing a bit as I did so. It was surprisingly difficult not to be able to wipe ones face and my hands struggled to perform the act a few times before I managed to quell them. Truth be told, I was still quite drunk.

"What's going on?" I said, as if I couldn't tell.

"You're going on a journey."

"I see that. I just.. Wanted to know why.. What's going on, Davis?"

"Tying up loose ends, Tony. Nothing personal."

"Ok." That made sense. I was absolutely the fall guy and now I had to disappear. How could I be so stupid not to understand that? But why was I doing a Neuro?

"Who is this.. Let's see.. N.. Nick?"

"Nash."

"Nash. Ok. How'd he die?"

"Suicide."

Of course. For all of his science, he was deep down, still a poet. I fell silent, my chirpy self-denial dribbling out of me, as I watching Davis go about his business, ticking off the procedures and checks one by one. God, it was so weird. Eventually, I was helped from the chair, wrists temporarily freed and assisted and strapped firmly onto the gurney, my head duly clamped.

"Davis, this bed, where did it come from?"

"It's an old prison rig they built for lethal injection."

Had Sammie been behind all this? All the Neuros? He leant over and checked my pulse, then my pupils for dilation. "Davis, it's a shame you never got to do this. I woulda done this for you. I coulda done it."

This stopped him for a second. "I know. I believe you. I just.. Can't."

" So what happens here?"

"You go in, you don't come out." He turned his face away to hide his emotion, to pull himself together and carry on. "I'm sorry. Bye, Tony."

So this was how I was going to go. Well, it took away the guesswork. And there were worse ways.

"Given the choice, I woulda chosen a pig in the bluebells, but... not so bad."

"Yeah, not so bad." He agreed.

"I'll do the debrief.."

"Shut up, Tony." He squared the needle and pushed. As he did so, there was a crash and all the lights went out.

33

The moment I woke up, the first thing to strike me was the stink of bad breath. This was followed by intrusively bright lights and the inquisitive face of a man with the bad breath. It still took me a while to work out where I was.

"Can you tell me your name?" He breathed.

"Anthony Pesic."

With that, he withdrew and I realised there were a great many people in the room. Another face loomed in, this time not so close.

"Anthony Pesic, I'm arresting you on suspicion of murder..." It was ridiculously easy to tune out. All I could think was, if I didn't find a toilet soon, there'd be an embarrassing mess that someone else was going to have to clean up. I interrupted.

"Can I use the washroom? Please?"

The officer paused and looked behind him. Obviously a

decision above his pay grade. A bottle was brought forward and handed to me. Well, if that was all I was going to get, it would have to do, but it was a bit of a come down from the safe house. If my bladder had been any less stressed, it might have been hard to relax, with so many people observing.. A couple of hours rest and then a pair of visitors, this time they announced themselves as FBI. Well, this was going to go well.

"What can you tell us about the AY-ZEE cyberworm?"

"I don't know anything about it. I'm a bit of a luddite when it comes to computers, I'm afraid."

"You deny all knowledge?"

"Well, yeah."

"You don't own, or never owned a Subatech 500Gig hard drive?"

"I don't think so. I had a Mac and a little hard drive to back that up, but I left that in London. The drive, I mean."

"Do you have any reason to suspect why anyone else might try to set you up for a major cybercrime?"

"No not really."

"You're aware of the severity of this crime?"

"I watched the news. I know someone took out a Wall Street company of some sort. That they attacked the banks and they hit... you guys, but beyond that, I don't. I wouldn't really understand what they did, or how they did, even after you explained it. I've never had any dealings in finance, or computer... software technology. It's not my thing."

"What about murder. Is that your thing?"

"Ok, so I don't know where you found me. But if it was at the lab, the Cryonics lab, then they're the guys you want. Yes, I went and picked up two cases, but I didn't know what was in them was at all dodgy.. Illegal. I was just doing what

I'd been asked to do." I said.

"So you didn't think picking up two frozen heads in a Walmart carpark and paying 150K in cash for them was at all dodgy?"

"Yes, it was dodgy. But I didn't know they were men hit for the purposes of what we were doing."

"Asked by who?"

"Davis. The guy in the lab sticking a needle in my skull.."

"You realise one of the guys you decapitated was an FBI agent?"

"No, I didn't... nor did I decapitate anyone."

"Let me..." Said the other guy. "What exactly were you doing, Mr Pesic?"

"I don't think you would believe me, even if I told you."

They looked at each other.

"Try us."

After asking for a drink of water, I started at the beginning, leaving out everything about the delivery of the hard drive, just starting at the point of working as a security guard for the lab. Thereafter, pretty much, everything was verbatim. When I'd finished, there was a pause.

"Would you repeat all of that and then sign a document verifying that all you said here was the truth?"

"Sure."

I imagine, shortly after that conversation, my laptop, the lab, the safe house, my London flat and Sammie's place were all taken apart. In the meantime, I expected to be transferred somewhere high-security, to await my trial.

34

My pre-dawn arrival at jail went unannounced and I was hurried through to solitary, but still word got out that America's Most Wanted was within their domain. Other guys in adjacent cells barked out in excitement, though with the echoes, I couldn't discern what was being said. The next day, prisoners in the exercise yard above me were shouting down to my grill. I was a celebrity. And how.

"You ain't nobody til somebody shoot you." The first comment I got upon passing another cell. I guess it was a backhanded compliment that they felt they had to say it in the first place, but it wasn't particularly settling to hear.

"You know this..?" Said my guard.

"It's a quote?"

"Biggie Smalls. You know him?"

"The rapper.."

"The rapper. Tha's right. You' get along jus' fine."

Well I hadn't quite been shot, but near as damn it. My time in jail turned out to be all about keeping me away from other inmates, who might want to take a pop at me. For the time being at least, the FBI wanted me alive, firstly to give them time to find out what I knew and then to dispose of as they would wish and not as someone else would. Vengeance was a big deal in America.

How had I not seen that Davis was Sammie's man all along? He even told me, that day up at the Redwoods, but I hadn't seen it. God, he must have enjoyed that so much. Just another bitch.

I guess that was the real enemy in here, down in your hot, stinking concrete box, all you had to look at was yourself. Failings; replaying over and over what went wrong, the what if's and if only's. Everything, every weapon, every negative feeling had nowhere to go, except inward. All around me, men were left to tear themselves apart until there was nothing left. Just a hard shell for others to break themselves on, should they get too close.

The FBI came back for another go. It was a long, laborious affair where I basically had to repeat all that I had already told them. But this time, they had a lot more information for me to chew over, plus I had also been assigned a lawyer. They'd drawn a blank on the computer crime, which to me was an obvious conclusion, as I'd had nothing to do with it and, how ever exhaustive their search, they'd never find anything that told them any different. But they'd changed their angle a little.

"Who made the cyberworm for you?"

"I didn't order it. I didn't make it. You need to talk to Davis. Whatever I don't know, he'll be able to fill in the blanks. Him and Sammie."

"So Sammie ordered the hit on our guy, had him frozen and he's also responsible for the worm."

"Right."

"So why are your fingerprints on the casing?"

"I don't know. I've not see this drive, I've never use this drive. Surely you know by now, it's never been even connected to me, or my laptop." I said.

"Why would this Sammie set you up?"

"Well, he needs for someone to take the rap, no?"

"We checked out the address you gave us, up in Topanga?"

"And..?"

"Is this Sammie?" He showed me a picture of an all-American couple in their sixties.

"No.."

"You're sure?"

"Perfectly."

"It's their home."

"What?"

"The residence you gave us, this address, is theirs."

"Jesus."

We looked at each other and they shared a glance.

"But.. They only live there for six months of the year, the rest of the year, they're travelling."

"So Sammie.. Took it over.."

They paused, determined not to look at each other, but failing dismally.

"What else can you give us on this guy, Sammie?"

"You need to speak to Davis. Why aren't you talking to him? Sammie ordered the Neuros, Davis sorted them out."

"Is this Davis?" He held up another picture, this time, a police mugshot.

"Yeah, that's Davis, the scientist, you must know this. He

can't hide his expertise. Speak to him. Are you speaking with him? What's he saying?"

"His name is Hernandez and he committed suicide in his cell, two days ago."

I looked at the pair of them. Of course he fucking did.

"Well, I've told you everything I know. You have to piece all that together with the fact that Davis, or Hernandez, was busy doing whatever he was eminently qualified to do, long before I arrived on the scene. You can also see I haven't got all the millions or billions that got sucked out of the international banks. You've seen my offshore account. You know that. There's someone else out there, someone well-versed in computing and big money."

"Yeah, well let me tell you this, wise-ass. 'Someone' masterminded a billionaire playtoy, using dead skulls and cocaine. One of our guys is dead~ used as one of these playthings and you were caught not only with the proceeds but in the act of taking one of those trips. 'Someone' attempted to make the FBI look pretty fuckin' stupid and it's got your fingerprints all over it. Be very clear, the banks and Wall Street want all this to go away. Period. All of this, coupled with a fake Swiss passport magicked out' your ass, a bag of loose change and an offshore bank account, containing 15-million bucks.. Something tells me a jury isn't gonna see everything the way you see it. Ok? So unless you magic 'Sammie' out of your ass aswell and pretty damn fast, then I would suggest that this passenger is fast coming to the end of the line.." His friend stood up to restrain him as his spittle started to spatter my face. "He was my fucking friend ok? You sick fuck. He was my friend, not a... trip for some rich prick to get his rocks off, reliving how he got murdered -in cold blood, you hear me?!" He wiped his mouth and slammed out of the room.

As I shuffled in ankle and wrist bracelets back to my cell, my lawyer, who'd said nothing at all for the entire interview, now got verbal diarrhoea in his haste to vacate the oppression of the situation in which he found himself.

"The press know nothing at all about the err.. About the Neuros, the cryonics and the 'trips', you understand? This is all news. But, come the court case, they're gonna hear everything about it. I think you need to prepare yourself for that. People are pretty sensitive about the dead, about caring for the dead, but more particularly about the sanctity of Christ and preserving, ahh.. that is.. preserving the memory.. respecting the dead. What I'm saying is they aren't going to like this much. With Hernandez gone, well... you're gonna be taking the brunt of it. So just prepare yourself." Before he managed to go on and explain exactly how I might go about that preparation, he was gone.

I was being lined up for Corcoran Prison, home to Charles Manson, family-killer Dana Ewell, Phillip Garrido the rapist who'd kidnapped a girl aged 11 and kept her hostage for 18 years and mass-murderer, Juan Corona. Despite my fake passport, I seemed to have sorted out my short stay visa issues.

35

The trial was a true spectacle. A high-budget, all singing, all dancing affair. Even though I'd seen myself -my story- depicted on the news, nothing really prepares you for the wattage of the spotlight, when it actually falls on you. I was bundled from armoured van to court with a blanket over my head, but it did nothing to protect me from the furore, the hunger of press hounds wanting a word, a look, just footage, hopefully of my face. Screaming, shouting, rammed against fences and gates, a single, multi-limbed animal, bristling with lenses, lights and microphones.

And the lawyer was right. Once the mystery surrounding the cryonics lab had broken, well, if I thought it was a raging river before, someone opened the floodgates. It went from hushed disbelief in the courtroom, to utter pandemonium outside. At any one time there were between four and seven helicopters circling whichever building I was in. I was shuttled across state lines, shoved in a succession of cells, whilst the authorities struggled with the pressure and the very real possibility that I would be killed before I even reached the verdict.

America blew a gasket. It didn't matter what I was or wasn't guilty of, any voice, any argument I may have had was lost in the tsunami of revulsion I faced, as the families of Frank, George, Harry, Ivan, John, Kirk and Marco were wheeled out, each in turn. The circumstantial evidence, the fact that none of the money from the Swift heist had been recovered from my accounts, the fact that I was filmed paying for the head of a man protecting the integrity of the United States of America and I had made millions in a few months from all of this, meant the nation's opinion was undivided. It was best I spoke as little as possible and let the machine, the circus, the US version of Roman entertainment makes its steady crescendo and turn its collective thumb down to hover a short time over the switch of my lethal injection.

"Have you reached a verdict?"

"Yes, your honour."

"And was your verdict unanimous?"

"It was, your honour."

Once convicted, it made things a little easier for them as this meant penitentiary, not jail. I was transferred first to Folsom, a prison built from granite hewn by it's earliest inmates, but I didn't stay long. Two guards were taken hostage and three inmates died in the ensuing violence, which took 53 hours to resolve, as the inmates themselves rioted their displeasure at the un-Americanness of my crimes. It was decided that I be removed and word put out that I was going to be taken to Terre Haute, a high security facility with its own Death Row, the Special Confinement Unit, opened in 1999. The Oklahoma bomber Timothy McVeigh had been incarcerated here, before his life was extinguished by lethal injection. The authorities went to great lengths, sending a heavily escorted, bombproof wagon all the way from Folsom Prison in California, to Terre Haute Pen, just over the Illinois border, in Indiana. Meanwhile, I was secreted in a decidedly unprotected mail van thirty minutes later, at the same time as three other prison vehicles, travelling in four different directions.

The ruse worked and I was installed in Havasu Lake Penitentiary, Arizona, without being rumbled by any press. I'd been resident for three days before word got out. By the time the maelstrom arrived, 'Lake Pen' were ready for it and, oddly, although there was plenty of disquiet from some quarters within the prison itself; it being a place for the real outsiders, many of them seemed to celebrate the fact I'd been put there, as it reinforced the point that they were in the institution with the real, Grade-A crims.

I was banged up in a cell of my own, with just 28 others on our own Death Row. Being a relatively new and purpose-built installation, it was a cleaner, quieter place than any I'd witnessed earlier. I was also allowed to mix with the other inmates, although in limited fashion and always under close guard. I soon learned though not to get too involved and keep myself to myself. Without exception, they all wanted something from me, something I was unable to give, as I didn't really understand it myself. But it was to do with the pecking order. Simply by my being there, I had taken top spot. How did I know this? Well, I was getting something of the order of 12,000 letters a week, from all corners of the globe. I was assigned first a PA, then an agent to field the calls for all the offers that were coming in. Producers wanting the rights to my film, documentary makers wanting to interview me. Ghostwriters to write my story. Then there were the women just wanting my flattened toothpaste tubes. Anything I had, anything I used had a value, the used toilet rolls, books I read, food wrappers, toenail clippings.. They were all worth thousands of dollars.

After the first twenty or so, I stopped trying to keep up. I didn't read many, I didn't answer any. This was for two reasons. If they were communications from people I knew, I knew I would find them upsetting. And if they were from fans or nutters, then they were seeking only to find meaning in their own lives and this was something I wouldn't be able to give. There was one notable exception my PA suggested I should read. It was a letter enclosed within another, both handwritten. The first being from my uncle.

Dear Antonio

When I gave the reading at your father's funeral, little did I suspect you would take my advice so literally. I cannot condone what you have done. Only you will fully understand the reasons why you have done these things. Although, I remember your father had a wild side and it wasn't your mother that tamed him, it was the day you were born.

Anyway, these days it's never even possible to work out where the truth lies, we can only read what it says in the papers, like everyone else. Your aunt didn't want me to write, but if this letter reaches you, I just wanted to let you know, whatever you did or didn't do, you will always be loved.

Take care of yourself, my boy. I'll be thinking of you.

Uncle Smudge

My PA was right. The letter managed to destroy me and it took a couple of days before I could read the other one, from my neighbour, Ruth:

Dear Anthony

I'm enclosing a letter for you. I hope they get through. There's been a few others, but they look like they can wait.

We've had two weeks of rain, which has been very hard on the veggies and your gutter sprang a leak, above the kitchen window. You'll be pleased that we managed to get a local handyman to sort it out, but it needed a long ladder, which was very difficult to get into the back garden. He came very highly recommended though, so we trusted him to do a good job. It seems to be fixed and I've used him myself since to sort out my kitchen drawer and put the door back on the wardrobe in the spare bedroom. The cost of the guttering was £90. I hope that is alright.

Best wishes,
Ruth

It was so like her not to mention the glaringly obvious. I had really doubted I'd be able to get any money to her, though.

And the women. Tens of thousands of them, with locks of hair, with photos, with underwear. They loved me, they wanted my children, they wanted to know what I liked, whether I liked them, they wanted sex in my cell, they wanted to have sex with their best friends, with strangers for my gratification, if that was what I wanted. They wanted to sit at my feet and listen. To cook for me, feed me, bathe me, massage me, stroke me, cut my hair, shave my body... And they didn't stop. Many wrote hundreds of letters, a letter a day, from the first day they found out I was secured in Lake Pen. My sex gurus would have been so proud. Surprised, but proud. Probably envious. But I knew it wasn't me these women wanted, they were after something I'd become, which was nothing to do with me. Something impossibly dangerous and bad, who'd rewritten the definition of what it meant to go too far, hanging up out of reach, somewhere between trophy and myth.

36

Days and nights soon lapsed inevitably into routine. Unlike the rest of the prison, things were more relaxed for the 29. I'd get up around eight, go for breakfast, grab a bag lunch I could take back to my cell and have a nap for a few hours. Then I'd take lunch on my own, have another nap, read something, the latest list from my PA, maybe a book, maybe some letters, do a limited exercise routine - not for any reasons of fitness, but just to stop my legs from keeping me awake by aching at night, having sat inactive for so much of the day. Then I'd go for dinner and refuse invitations to play chess, drafts or chat overly with my fellow inmates.

In the ensuing weeks after my trial, the world stock exchanges turned upside down, as I said. Stainless steel, Cryonics in general, real estate, everything to do with the process went sky-high. If I had done nothing else, I had released the genie from the bottle; that there was indeed Life after Death. And if it was only ten seconds right now, who was to say in ten- or fifty years time, science wouldn't have overcome the hurdles that so far defeated Davis?

From time to time, usually when pushed to do so by my agent, my PA might flag something up, like 'would I like to meet such-and-such producer, writer or filmmaker..?' My answer would always be No. As a convicted prisoner, I wasn't allowed to profit from the story I'd gone down for. I didn't see why they should. Someone would make the story once I was gone and besides, no one was really interested in my story anyway, they just wanted some sort of affirmation of the story they felt they already knew, the one that had become legend. It was only at this point, after another short exchange with my PA, that something shifted. I'd rejected another proposal by a biographer from New York. He specialised in Death Row inmates and had made a good living from it, too.

"Why don't you write it yourself, Tony? You're so worried no one wants your story, so write it. I would. What else is there to do in there?"

She was right, of course. What better to be doing than chronicling the Tale of Tony Peso?

With a few enquiries, I was afforded access to a basic word-processor and, after a few false starts came up with an opening I was pleased with but, after a couple of stabs, gave up with it. Instead, I took to writing through the night, in my cell, with pencil, on paper. It was a lot more immediate, I didn't need to slow my progress looking for keys. I could write when I wanted to and not be cornered by specific hours. I also wanted to write without the sense that what I wrote was being pored over by the Feds, the moment I walked out of the room. I wanted to write with the freedom that it would only be read once I'd gone. I sincerely doubted this would be the case, but it was important to me, in the doing of it to believe this to be the case. Then I could write the whole truth.

I wrote fast. I wrote so fast, I worried I wouldn't be able to decipher my own scrawl when I got to the other end, but my PA continued only to encourage me, so I just carried on, aware time was limited, I had a lot to say and I didn't need to be getting in my own way; I wasn't going to appeal my sentence. There would be no prolonging, no delay, no extra series for the audience to devour before the finale. Once I started, it was a relief to actually let it all out, having seemingly given a vow of silence over the whole affair since my conviction. The term 'deadline' had first been coined at Folsom Prison in the days of construction, prior to 1920, by which time the outer walls were completed. The 'deadline' was chalked on the ground and anyone stepping across it would be instantly shot by the watchtower guards stationed at each corner.

My commencement of writing brought with it a willingness to accept visits. This cheered my agent up no end, as he'd thought he was on a absolute gold-plated winner until I point-blank refused all comers. He put it down to the fact that I had faced up to and accepted the fact that I was going to die soon and my ego was too big not to get across my version. But my reason was more straightforward than that. I wanted to know what they saw going up on screen, or in a book. I needed to find out what would sell, what they believed to be 'the sizzle'. It was very instructive and actually completely altered the way I wrote and what I chose to focus in on. They went away delirious, with a 'so, maybe we can work together' and my agent was delighted too. I think only my PA suspected what was going on, but if she did, she didn't say anything.

It was on one of these days I got the call to go for another meeting. I finished my lunch and, accompanied in standard ankle and arm chains by two guards, I jingle-jangled through six locked gates to the booth. Booths were separated by a glass partition and you spoke to the other person by use of a phone. A couple of times, my interviewers had asked for a less formal setting, as in their view I wasn't a dangerous murderer known for my uncontrollable temper. I think they felt if the setting were more informal, they might be able to apply more by way of persuasion, but from the start, the Warden put his foot down and banned it, outright.

I sat down and waited a few minutes, a little preoccupied and wondering whether this one would provide anything at all useful, when a woman slid in quickly and at an angle, leaning down to deposit her bag and then sat up, flicking her hair as she did so, to reveal the face of Erin.

37

I sat silent, phone in hand, not taking in the apparition before me, before finally saying "Erin."

Her right hand hovered nervously over the flap of her jacket pocket as she cleared her throat and then spoke.

"Hello, Tony. I don't want to say much. I just wanted to see you.."

She then dove into the pocket she'd been toying with, retrieved and unfolded a piece of paper, then pressed it on the glass for me to read.

"Ok.." I said.

Dearest Tony

I'm hoping you'll get to read this. I'll be putting myself in considerable danger to enable this to happen, but I do it of my own choice. Sammie pulls all the strings and we are all puppets in his show, knowingly, willingly, or not.

When you dropped into his lap, he believed it nothing less than a sign from God. For it was your father he held a vendetta for. In the early days before Sammie was born, Mamad and he sparred, and Mamad lost. But he never forgave, he never forgot and he never let his son forget either.

Tony, I have love for you and as you also know, I can't bear injustice of any kind. It tore at my heart to see you used so blindly, led by the nose so callously, but you didn't help yourself. We are all our father's children, are we not? And there is something in you that makes you easy to manipulate, to use. You have to change this. I knew you took Mamad's Neuro. Sammie needed you to fall for me, to confide in me. To stay longer than you wanted to, in order to make it all work. He knew his father would approve if, even in death, he was instrumental in finally gaining his revenge.

You didn't take the first Neuro, Sammie did. He had already experienced and understood what happened when you took that trip and Davis was always his man. Sammie had those two men killed and their heads delivered only to trap you. But perhaps you know this.

So know only that I tried to love you, but my heart died with Mamad and somehow, briefly, you were the last vestige of the man I gave my life to, for better or worse. After that, I didn't care if I lived or died. Perhaps that's wrong of me, whose to judge?

And this is Sammie's parting gift to you. He told me to write this letter, needing you to understand. So you know why you are here.

I only hope you can find it in your heart to forgive me.

He will always win.

Her eyes followed mine down the page as I took it all in. I looked at her only twice, once with the reveal that my father was so involved and again, when she declared she didn't care whether she lived or died. I'm not sure when I started to cry.

When she was sure I'd finished, she crushed the letter back into her pocket. We looked at each other for a short while, then she put her hand up on the glass and I immediately joined her there, listening only to her breath down the phone.

"It's really good to see you, Tony."

"Is your name Erin?"

She nodded.

"But Sammie? Is not Sammie.."

She smiled apologetically, then slowly pulled the handset from her ear and hung up the phone.

"Farzhad." She mouthed silently, through the glass.

And then she left, her handprint evaporating as she went.

"Erin.."

I don't remember stumbling back to my cell. I did attempt to write though, as soon as I got there, to reconstruct the letter, word for word, as much as I could recall, going back and adding sentences as I pictured the print on the glass infront of me, even though every line remembered was like a blade stabbed into my heart. And so I scribed the last few lines to my manuscript:

The journey from my cell to the waiting room is 38 steps. From that cell to the chamber itself, only another nine, without shackles.

I would be made to lie down on a bed and six robust leather straps used to render me immobile. A needle would be inserted into my arm, which for some reason they deem necessary to wipe with alcohol, so preventing infection. The bed would then be raised, so those in the gallery could watch, as three separate cylinders emptied into me one by one, the first to make unconscious, the second to arrest both muscle and lungs and the third to stop the heart.

I have gone through phases of dwelling on it, but have also made a good go of managing to completely block it out for large periods of time. Not really dwelling on what it meant, just the fact that it was the end and, unlike most people, I knew with some reliability when it would happen~ the day before the anniversary of my mother dying and through a very similar process when she euthanased. I did ask that it be delayed a day, just for that symmetry but, true to form, my wishes were ignored.

You know my name. And I am soon to witness my very own last ten seconds...

The End

38

As I lay half-dozing in my cell, realising I really wasn't too far away from the place I'd not long ago stood, taking in the desert and deciding I didn't want to stay in Arizona, if I could help it, my cell neighbour chimed in.

"Dude. You hearin?"

"What?"

"Drug company's refusin the drug."

We all knew what the drug was. All the other illicit drugs available within the prison had their own pet names, but not the one used as the lethal injection. This was news. I'd heard the case in a different state, where a man had been saved the death penalty at the last moment not through a reprieve, but because the prison had managed to procure the wrong drugs and so had needed to postpone the event. I didn't know if it had subsequently gone ahead at a later date. I didn't think this setback would do much to stop them snuffing me out, but it was interesting.

"What they gonna do?" I said, rousing myself.

"Use bleach, probly."

It was this conversation that made what followed less surprising. I'd finished my manuscript the day before and didn't want to look at it any more. All I was doing as I did so was face the knowledge that it was all at an end, my hands would start shaking as an uncontrollable urge to cry pitifully overtook me, so I preferred to sleep if I could.

Just gone noon, whilst most of the inmates were at lunch, three officers arrived at my cell.

"Bag whatever you want. You're on the move."

Grabbing my manuscript, I stuck it in my pillowcase and left it on the floor by my feet, then nodded to the officer through the door. There was nothing else I wanted. I then stood, hands against the wall, as I awaited the chains.

"Where am I going?"

No answer.

Stuffed pillowcase under my arm, I was escorted all the way out, to be met by the Warden, suffering in the harsh, midday sun. His disappointment was palpable, as if it were somehow my fault.

"I wanted to watch you go."

There wasn't much I could say to that. I looked at him, wondering whether there was anything of more interest. Having scuffed around in the dust with his toe a while, he recovered himself enough to continue.

"Oklahoma has no such issues. They still have the firing squad but, unfortunately, you will be receiving Nitrogen hypoxia as scheduled and not a day later." He stepped away and I was helped into the back of a small van, this time on my own, albeit still heavily manacled.

"Too good for the likes of you." He said, as the door banged the light out.

Again, I exited the prison gates with two dummy vehicles, in case anyone had got wind of my departure. As we filed past the outer fence, there was quite a crowd gathered, but not as big as was expected in a couple of days, the date of my execution. I wondered how many would find out I wasn't actually there and I wondered why they cared.

On my own, I bounced about on a very hard seat, unable to sit comfortably with the chains, but alone to my thoughts. We'd been going for over an hour when we pulled off the highway and drew to a halt. The back doors opened and I was assisted down. It seemed early for a loo-break, but was grateful to stretch my legs and catch some new landscape. What greeted me was a large, silver wagon with blacked out windows. As I looked, the back door opened. I glanced back at my armed prison driver, but he'd turned away, intent on lighting a cigarette, so I scuffed towards the proffered opening. As I did so, an unseen driver gunned the engine and, with some difficulty, I piled into the back. Taking a bench seat, the door was slammed behind me and we were off. Immediately, the door-closer set about my chains, slipping a protective plate of steel between my wrist and manacle, then pulling on some heavy leather gloves, swift use of an angle grinder soon cut me free. I nodded my thanks to my new best friend, but he busied himself under the seat, shortly to pass me a bottle of water and a clothes parcel. In it, a light pair of trousers, a white cotton shirt, some sandals and what turned out to be a billowy, black burqa. Needing no further encouragement, I divested myself of prison garb and pulled them all on, fiddling around with the headpiece to get the eye slit right.

"Where are we going?" I ventured.

There was no answer forthcoming and, the rear of the van being separated from the driver, I contented myself with smiling to myself and looking out of the window. We travelled on for another few hours, over the border into New Mexico and then pulled off the main drag and shortly into a dirt side track. Here, we changed vehicles again, this time a dark green G-Wagon, the difficulty of my chains surpassed in negotiating the long, full skirts of my new attire combined with the restricted vision. I got myself sorted and waved my grateful goodbyes to the van.

"How are you, my friend?"

With all the difficulties of my burqa, falling over my sandals and hem and the slit of my headpiece now all askew, I hadn't realised I had company.

"Emir."

"How does it feel to be a free man once again?"

"Emir, don't ask me why, but I had my suspicions it must be you. No one else has the panache that you do."

"You flatter me. But thank you, it's always gratifying to be appreciated. We have a few hours to Albuquerque, where my plane awaits. Are you hungry?"

I smiled my response and he produced a large tray of meze dishes.

"Emir, you realize, I can never repay you..."

"What is a life without risk? Come to that, what is a life without friends?"

Even so, it seemed extreme to me.

"You risked a great deal to save me. You still are.."

"But this can all wait. Wait until we're over international waters, at least."

I waded into the meze.

"Wait. How did you pull this off?"

It was the question he'd been waiting for.

"Well, breaking into a prison, it's such a messy business.. Too many unknown factors.. You have to involve all sorts of people you don't want to involve. Pay criminals.." He shook his head with distaste. "I couldn't decide what to do and time was running exceedingly short. I refused to think about it any more, I'm going about my business and then it hits me, from an unexpected place."

"What does?"

"I'm looking at a magazine with you on it in one hand and staring at the answer on a piece of paper in my other."

I awaited the impending enlightenment.

"One of our many majority holdings is in two of the bigger pharmaceutical companies. I call a meeting and say I no longer want our company to have dealings in executions. It was easy to argue, brand profile.. Negative public image.. so forth..."

Wow. I thought he'd simply heard the news that the drugs companies had pulled out, not that he'd actually instigated it.

"A little research and I find Arizona has no capability for another form of execution, they'll have to move you. Of all executions, America's Most Wanted, this one has to be seen to be done right. Right?"

"Right.."

"It was easy to see that a simple thing like this would jeopardise the whole execution. A few calls down the chain to the prison Warden and he would open all the doors and gates, willingly. He would deliver you wherever I needed."

"It's brilliant, Emir. Brilliant." And I couldn't fault it, it really was.

"You are the first person I have ever sprung from prison. I must say I enjoyed the experience, but it was disappointingly simple, once I applied my mind to it." He said.

'He that believeth in me, though he were dead, yet shall he live: And whosoever liveth and believeth in me shall never die.' If ever there was a man to believe in, as far as I was concerned, it was this one.

39

Waved onto the apron, we pulled up adjacent to Emir's plane. Not the expected 747, but a much smaller 18-seater. By now, Emir had gently informed me that what I needed to do was move far more slowly when manoeuvring myself in my new get up. This gave the time necessary to ensure I didn't fall over anything, lose a sandal, or boggle my eye-line so I could no longer see where I was going. As I took my seat, grateful I'd negotiated the stairs without mishap, the door was snapped shut behind us and we taxied off to the runway. As we took off, with some relief, I removed the headdress and, as we plateaued above 30,000ft, received the offered flute of champagne, turning to Emir in salutation.

"To drugs." He pre-empted.

I couldn't help but grin at this. I took a sip and then returned "To good friends."

His turn to smile, he drank to that.

"Please, if you wish, I can get you someone to help you out of that burqa, but I just ask that you put it on once more, when we land so we can safely transfer you.."

"Of course." I said.

Unbuckling myself, I retreated to the back and extricated myself without help. They really were the most restrictive items of clothing. Returning to my seat, I realised I hadn't actually felt free until this moment, standing in ordinary, well-fitting clothes, in the confines of a private jet. Prior to that, it was the burqa that had deprived me of the sensation.

We flew on to O'Hare and, having successfully transferred to the 747, after a short wait, lifted off and set course for Dubai. Showered and fed, I lay back in the luxury of my now familiar cabin, looking around it with new eyes. I honestly never thought I would ever be seeing this again. Infact, I hadn't thought about it at all, so comprehensive was the knowledge that to do so was simply gratuitous birching. But here, now, PoB, it was an extraordinary feeling.

We were somewhere over the Atlantic at the hour of my planned execution. Emir turned on the news to see what had occurred.

"His execution went ahead, not in Lake Havasu Penitentiary, Arizona, as many thought, but in Oklahoma. The reason for this well, we can go over live to Steve, standing outside, among the crowds assembled at Lake Pen, What can you tell us, Steve?"

"Well, I can tell you, there are more people here than anyone can remember for an execution in living memory. A huge police presence needed as you can see, to keep the pro-life supporters away from those that are very pleased to see the back of Anthony Pesic. What caught all of them unawares though, is the fact that, as you have just learned, Tony Peso was secreted out of here at some point in the last few days, we aren't sure when.. and taken over state borders to Oklahoma, where the death penalty can actually be administered in one of several ways. Now, since the use of lethal injection is being ruled out over several states, we understand that Anthony Pesic was gassed, at dawn this morning, his body immediately cremated and his ashes scattered in a secret location. John."

"Thankyou Steve.. Well, there you have it. Anthony Pesic, Tony Peso, America's Most Wanted, has been summarily executed for murder, away from the public eye and his ashes scattered.."

I looked at Emir, not quite believing what I was watching.

"Well, it's not that surprising is it? I can't see how they would admit that you had escaped death row in a high security prison. There would be rioting in the streets."

I looked back at the screen, shots of candle-clutching pro-life picketers embracing each other, grief-stricken at my passing. It was incredible.

"So. Now you are truly free."

I looked at Emir, still not comprehending.

"You no longer exist. You can travel anywhere. Do anything.. Within reason." He chortled."But first, you have to meet my friends. You are a hero in Dubai... across the Middle East... anyone who can do so much to puncture the arrogance of America is welcomed with open arms in any Arab state." He said. "But first, we have some work to do. Are you willing to help me, Tony?"

"Of course. Whatever I can do.."

"Good. Let us get down to business. What can you tell me about this man, Sammie? Anything, any information you may have, however small, it could help me track him down."

"Ok, well, his name isn't Sammie. It's Farzhad."

Emir stopped in his tracks. "Farzhad. Farzhad who?"

"I don't know. I don't know anything about him. The house he lived in wasn't even his."

"Tony, my friend, you know far more than you believe you do. Just take your time to process. Can you jot down anything that occurs to you? Anything he said, anything Davis said about him, anything at all about who this man is."

"His father was called Mamad... he drove a Ferrari, at least I think he did, I think it was his. It felt like it was his..."

"Do you know the licence plate? Anything?"

I shook my head, disconsolate.

"That's ok, what else?"

I wracked my brain, trying to remember the conversation we'd had among the trees. But he had been the one asking all the questions and I had sung like a canary.

"He's Persian and probably well-known in that community. Someone must know him.." Persisted Emir.

"There was a restaurant.."

"What about it?"

"Well, it may be nothing, but.. We went for a trip, out to see the giant redwoods, then came back and stopped at a superb sushi restaurant. And the maitre D seemed to know him, as if he was a regular."

"Where was this restaurant?"

"Over towards Century City.. Ze, no.. Zo. Zo Sushi. Sushi Zo."

"That's good enough. Well done. We need his surname." He said.

A lightbulb went on.

"I have a hunch I can find out, if I can just get to my father's papers. They're in my flat, in London."

Emir took a few seconds."You can't go there, that really is too difficult."

"I have a neighbour, we can ask her?"

"Again too fraught. Why would you be wanting to go through your fathers papers, from beyond the grave?"

"I'm sorry. I haven't got my head round my death yet. Not thinking straight."

"Would you be happy to allow me, one of my men to access..? If you tell me exactly where these papers are located, I can have them.. In less than six hours."

"I'm sure you can." I grinned.

"..If you will permit..?"

"Of course. But why are you intent on this man, all of a sudden? Emir, If it's for me, I don't need you to avenge me. I'm perfectly happy to have my life, my freedom." I said.

"I'm afraid you have me there, Tony. It is for entirely selfish reasons. You see, when the Swift system was hit, he went after the big money... the oil accounts, unsurprisingly."

"...Yours?"

Emir nodded.

Springing me from prison was making more sense. Emir seemed to read my thoughts.

"My friend. This way, I kill two birds with one stone, as you say. Win win." He smiled. "I wanted to help you before, but I was under immense pressure. By sending you back to America, I served all needs. We kept accord with the US.. we are seen to be doing the right thing... my people find out for certain you are telling the truth and, perhaps we flush out the true culprit. Too many people believed it was you, you understand?"

"Of course. Look Emir, if I can do anything to help you, you know I will."

"Perhaps you already have. I also feel I've been going about this all the wrong way. A man such as this, not used to wealth, real wealth, he's liable to stick his beak out in the more obvious ways."

"What do you mean?"

"You say he likes his Ferrari?"

I nodded.

"Let me see... he consulted an iPad. Boys and their toys... Here we are."

With the smallest glance, a steward was at his elbow and they spoke in earnest for a few minutes before the he slipped away.

"Excuse me. I am asking for the waiting list on the Gulfstream G650ER. I have started enquiries as to who might have his offshore holdings. And also collectible, Ferrari special editions... purchased, or going for auction in the near future. That should narrow the field." He said.

"Great."

"I also asked that someone make entry to your flat. Can you tell me where you think the papers are?"

"Of course. They're in a black, metal deed box. It should be sitting in the spare room, under the desk, on top of some boxes."

"Thank you." He said.

I did feel a slight pang. It had been wonderful to imagine that Emir was doing all of this for a friendship, from the goodness of his heart. But he was a businessman, after all was said and done. When would I learn?

"Whilst your man is there, could you do one thing.. Could he leave an envelope, addressed to Ruth, with £90 in it?"

"It's done. I'm curious. The process.. the trip. Do you know anything of it, or was Davis the surgeon?"

"Well, at one point I was training up, because Davis was going to be a passenger himself, I mean take a trip, but it never happened." I replied.

"So you never got to test your mettle."

"Not in that way, no." I smiled.

40

I wondered what to do with my book. It sat beside me, in the same stained pillowcase, looking very out of place in its new surroundings. I'd worked really hard to finish it, thinking it ended with my life at an end. But what now? Did I continue writing it? Who for? How would I ever publish it? And did I even want to?

Emir snapped me back into the present.

"Tea?"

I nodded. "Once we find him, what will you do?" I asked.

"What would you do?"

"Somehow deliver him to the Feds, I guess. They'll be pleased to meet him."

"I'm not so sure."

"What do you mean?"

"Well, it's an interesting point. You see, you have already paid for those crimes, both in the eyes of the people and the

FBI. Unless he's merely an accomplice.."

"So, what are you thinking?"

"We need to restore order.." He said, more as a thought than a response to me, however, nothing more was forthcoming.

I awoke in my chair to the announcement we were to start our descent into Dubai. Someone had wrapped me in a blanket and even removed my sandals. After a moment of getting my bearings, I made to get back into my burqa.

"Please sir, take a seat?"

"I'll need my burqa, won't I?" I responded.

"No sir, I don't think it will be necessary anymore."

I took to my seat again. A whole new world.

I'd dreamt I'd been walking up the street I lived on, to the local grocery. I didn't know the name of the man in the shop, but we always exchanged pleasantries, or at the very least a nod, if he was busy with another customer. But the main part of the dream was taken up with the walk up the hill at the end of my road. It was short but quite steep, giving a bit of a workout and a small sense of triumphant relief when you reached the top. In my dream, I was sucking in every fine detail, every discrepancy in texture and hue of the paving slabs, the stunted grass clumps and innocent flowers that had made an optimistic toehold in the cracks where the pavement met the wall. The overhanging Horse Chestnut, Ash and Balsam leaves and the way each neighbour along the street had dealt with their offensively large wheelie bins in small front gardens.

Coming to terms with the knowledge that I would never walk that walk again, never see anyone I knew, or who might know me, no family, no friends, not even the man in the local shop. No instant, warm recognition, borne of years. Again, I was forced to contemplate my grandmother's words; what was the point, if everyone I knew, everyone I loved, was gone? They were so integral- helped define me. This had never seemed to matter when I'd been wrapped up in my mad escapade. Just the fact that the shop, the sticking door to my flat, uncle Smudge and Ruth's cat Seamus existed, had been enough, enough to anchor me. Now, in their hearts and minds, I was dead and there was no coming back from that. No fairytale ending. What did one do when one was dead?

The landing was exceptionally soft. The aircraft didn't rattle and jerk like a plastic crate, it just had an assured firmness I'd not witnessed in any passenger jet.

"Refreshed?" Said Emir.

"I think I needed it." I said.

"What I think would be a good idea is if you stayed on the plane, at least for now. Treat it as a hotel. We haven't sorted out any papers for you and, just incase anyone is observing my movements, it just makes sense. We can sort out better arrangements when things settle."

"Sure." I said.

Emir and ten of his entourage left the aircraft and we then taxied to the outer airfield to park up. The engines finally dying, all the lights flickered briefly as the power was plugged into a ground source and a great many staff commenced the myriad tasks of servicing, taking luggage and turning the aircraft around in preparation for whatever came next. It was like standing backstage after a show.

I took a shower and then went to bed proper.

When I awoke, it was dark outside, but venturing out of the bedroom, I spied Emir, deep in thought at his office desk. He acknowledged my appearance with a finger, indicating he was in fact on a call. I retreated, rinsed my mouth and put a clean shirt and slacks on. By the time I went out again his attention was all mine.

"We seem to have a problem."

I raised my brow in question.

"Someone beat us to it. Your deed box is missing. It seems someone has done a thorough job of turning your flat over."

"Oh."

"It's not a burglary. Nothing else has been touched. But someone has gone in with that specific find in mind. Do you have any ideas?"

"I can only think Arif. Sammie-Farzhad's cousin. If Sammie went after that information, that's who he would have contacted. Whether Arif actually did it.. Or he sent someone. My sense is, Arif would have himself. Though. Unless it was the Feds. They must have sent someone in a while back."

"Where does he live, this Arif?"

"I'll need to jog my..." A few taps on a screen and a Streetview map of London showed me what I needed. "There. Euston. In that tower block, I don't know what it's called. Fourth floor. You turn right out of the elevator and it's the last door on the right. Sorry, I can't remember the address."

"No, that's good enough for me, if you're sure."

"Yes."

"Leave it with me. We may not need it. You'll be pleased to know we've had two results. Well, three really. We managed to track down your restaurant and got details of a business address from his card details."

"That's great."

"We also found him through the Gulfstream connection-so unimaginative that he should want what everyone else wants, but.. You can't teach class. We located one of his offshore accounts through the waiting list. I don't yet know how many accounts he has, whether he has all that money in one nest. I don't suppose he does, but there's also a limit to the number of organisations that can handle volume."

"So what are we going to do?"

"I've spent a good deal of thought on that. First of all we need to track him. Once we do that, we can find out where the money is. Then... well, let's see. How are you feeling?"

"A bit strange, if I'm honest."

"Yes, I can imagine. Have you decided what it is you want to do? Where you might go?"

"Am I able to access my money, do you think?"

"Where is it?"

"Zurich."

"Do the Feds know about it?"

"I'm not sure. I certainly never mentioned it. I told them of my offshore account, but I transferred a lump before I got picked up."

"Well, they will know you had somewhere, that will be on record, but whether they've found it... if they did it will be easy enough to find out." He reasoned.

"There's no need for them to be tracking that account now, I'm dead."

"Perhaps. The official story is you're dead, but the Feds know you're very much alive. If they have that account info, then they'll very much be monitoring it. How much is there?"

"Good point. About 25-mill." I said.

"Well, you don't need to worry for now."

"Thank you, Emir." I doubted it would be the last time I'd be saying that.

"Come my friend. I think it's time you let your hair down."

41

Rather than risk taking me off to some club or sprawling apartment, Emir brought the party to me. The plane was soon filled with a set of up-for-its, quite a mixed crowd with a sprinkling of western faces, but only amongst the women. If anyone did recognise me, no one seemed to react nor mention it, although I did look quite different from the images used in the news, having lost a bit of weight in the interim, prison food being what it was.

Emir stood at my elbow as I watched the girls dancing on the main floor.

"Any woman in the room Tony, who would you like to be introduced to?"

I had to smile. In none of the guru podcasts or forum conversations, did it ever suggest that the cast iron way to get laid was to be thrown your own party by a friendly Arab billionaire.

"Her..?" I said indicating a very sweet blonde in a shimmery silver dress. "And her.." Indicating her friend.

Emir gave a large smile and it was done.

I figured life was short, I'd been through a hell of a lot and being on Death Row, one was very short on opportunity, of the consensual kind at least. Besides, how often would I be in a situation such as this?

"Sherrin.. Nina, meet Joe. Joe's a good friend of mine."

"Hi. Where are you from?"

I had a moment's panic as I realised I was completely unprepared to reinvent myself on the spot, relieved Emir had already made a good start. But I really couldn't afford to play this too far from home, or I'd be undone.

"London. What about you?"

"South Africa." Said Sherrin.

"And you?"

"Bulgaria." Said Nina.

Ok. That was probably enough conversation. I allowed myself to be towed by Sherrin a couple of steps out of my comfort zone and started moving about to the music, happily sandwiched between the two of them, gyrating, enjoying the looks, smiles and flirts of perfumed hair. But it was a strange thing, as if I was removed from the situation I was in. Monopolising my thoughts was what was going on with Sammie, whether Emir had got a bead on him and what he would do with him once he did, which I had no doubt would happen.

I was all the better for champagne by the time the two of them chuckled me into my cabin and we all stripped off and landed on the silken play field.

"Have you done this before..?" I asked the pair of them.

My answer came in the form of coquetry and kisses. It

occurred to me I had no idea how to actually handle two women simultaneously and wondered what the etiquette might be, but they seemed perfectly at ease, so I let go and allowed myself to float with the flow.

"Tony..? We've found him." Said Emir.

I roused myself, feet sticking out from under my silk sheets to find my companions gone, humming in my ears, but thankfully no headache.

"Where is he?"

"On a flight back to LA. Get freshened up and we'll brunch.." He wheeled off the door jambe and I stared at the space he'd vacated. Only then did I pinpoint what the noise was. We were actually in flight.

I took a brisk shower, desperately trying to engage and get my business head on. My body ache reminding me of the night's escapades, in all sorts of good ways, unused as it was to being so stretched. By the time I'd dressed and joined Emir, a sumptuous spread of fresh fruits, breads, spreads, croissants, tea and coffee adorned the flower-strewn table, the chef in the galley awaiting my order, should I require eggs, bacon or pancake, or sausage. Emir, as usual, looked immaculate in a crisp shirt and tie.

"A good night?" He said.

"A very good night, thank you."

"A man so long in prison, he has at some point to answer his stronger needs, no?"

"Interestingly put."

"No complaints though?"

"Oh God, no. Lovely girls. Like models." I said, wondering what trouble might await them if I'd said otherwise.

"They are. Over on a photoshoot."

How silly of me. I ordered some scrambled eggs, suddenly wishing I'd got their numbers. "What are you thinking to do with Farzhad? How did you find him?"

"Through your lawyer.. Lawrence?"

"You've really been covering all bases."

"This man's a Persian and a creature of habit. I couldn't see him straying far. It's not as though he could go home."

"I guess not." I said, not having the faintest idea what was going on in Iran.

"And we drew a blank with your friend Arif. If he had your father's papers, he doesn't any longer. But it's of no consequence. We have him now. Farzhad Ghassemi."

"Ghassemi. So.. What next?" I said, buttering some deliciously fragrant rye bread.

"Yes. I have been thinking a great deal on that. We need to come up with a plan. We need to know where he has his money, this is priority."

"How might we find that out? I mean, presumably he has any number of accounts. He's not going to go to those big lumps that often, surely?"

"Exactly the situation. Until we know where they are, those big accounts and how many, we can't do anything other than track.. Try and find out more, where he lives. Maybe get a wire on him."

"I take it we're on our way to the US?"

"Indeed. But don't worry, my friend, everything is in hand." He said.

"I don't doubt it. Are those lychees..?"

42

Landing in LAX, I was thrown back to my Tobago trip with Erin. I wondered where she was right now, what she was doing. Perhaps we're always destined as a race to fall in love with the unattainable. It didn't make it any less real, or painful and I was glad I didn't still have her details, my phone buried somewhere in the bowels of the US prison system as it was.

Emir prepared to disembark, leaving me to my palatial prison cell.

"Do you know where he is?"

"No. We lost him. he'll resurface I'm sure, but it's not easy, he's a cautious man and looks to be taking precautions, whether he thinks he's being monitored or not.. We don't yet know where he lives. That is to say, we have a registered address for him, but he's not there. It'd be convenient to take a look at his diary. Know where he's going to be, but..."

"That's it." I said.

"What is? What is it, Tony?"

"Well, if he's anything like his father, then.. Then we can track him. Know where he's going to be..."

"You know his PA?"

"No, sorry.. Look. His father Mamad was cryonically frozen. I'm almost certain, being his father's son, he'll be planning exactly the same. He has to be.."

"So.."

"So, these days, the super rich.. Forgive me.. Americans? Well, they have it all prepped. They have the lab on standby, so if they die, the cryonics team step in and start the process as soon as they can."

"He has this?"

"I'd put money on it. They'll know where he is.. What his plans are, give or take."

"What's the name of this company? The one his father used?"

"Well, if it's still there after me and Davis put it on the map, Vermilion."

Entourage in tow, Emir swept off the plane.

"If you can bear to remain here a little longer. I promise to get you off soon."

"Emir..."

Striding a few short steps on concrete, he disappeared into the chaperoned door of a waiting Range Rover.

I turned to a screen and brought up Vermilion. They were indeed still there and had in fact expanded considerably, in the recent industry upturn I had been so instrumental in.

"Would sir care for a massage?"

I looked up, failing to focus on the stewardesses face, as I thought for a moment.

"Why not?" What else was there to do?

Comfortable on soft towels, the woman above piled into the knots in my neck and shoulders. She didn't mess about, her slight frame belying a determined strength.

What would happen when he found Farzhad? What would happen to me when he found him and had no more use for me? Was he really my friend, or a friend for long enough to serve purpose? It was a cliche of the rich to pick people of interest up and then drop them as quickly, once they got bored. Did I need an exit strategy? Might he even dispose of me~ I presumably knew too much.. And it would be pretty easy to do, considering I was already dead. God, if he wanted to be poetic about it, he could even have me delivered to the Oklahoma Prison I was meant to be going to, before he teleported me out. But what kind of an exit strategy? I was entirely dependent on him. I didn't even have a passport. I wouldn't last five minutes the moment I stepped off this aircraft, without his protection. And, although he might have just been scaring me up concerning access to my Swiss account, I could see his point. There was no way the FBI would let me go easily, having been found responsible for killing one of their own. My masseuse changed tack and climbed on top of me to walk down my back, bringing her sharp heels to bear on my back, her toes between my shoulder blades.

"Just breathe." She said.

I was trying.

Come to think of it, I really didn't know as much about Sheik M as I thought. Sure, I'd spent a great deal of time onboard his 747 one way or the other but, to my knowledge, I'd never met another member of his family, I didn't even now his proper name, if he was married, whether he was royalty or not, where he lived, not even the name of his company. On reflection, perhaps I didn't know too much. Perhaps it was also best to try and keep it that way; not get too nosey. He'd obviously engineered it how he wanted it for a reason. I didn't need to be going out of my way to force that issue. There was a sense with Emir that he enjoyed my company. We'd certainly come together on that riff of having a good time, of adventure and he must undoubtedly be surrounded with sycophants or work for a lot of the time. Perhaps he looked forward to just relaxing and having a laugh. I was of course dependent on him, but I had never begged anything of him, or been needy. All that I had received had been freely given, not asked for on my behalf. He'd definitely meant it in the debrief, when he'd come out the other side of his trip and been so open and grateful. Either way, I'd just have to wait and see. I wasn't really in a position to do otherwise.

I had a hankering to do all those things you really miss when couped up. A walk in the park on a fresh Autumn day. A dip in the ocean, breathing the view across Pembrokeshire from Snowdonia. Even jumping in a pool would have sufficed. I was surprised Emir hadn't worked out a way of having a swimming pool aboard a plane yet. Shoddy, really.

Feeling sorry for myself, I engaged in finding out what the England cricket team was up to when a phone was passed to me.

"Tony. You've done it again. We've got him. Cracked Vermilion, tracked him down."

"Great. What next?"

"Well, I've come up with a plan, if you're game..?"

"Sure."

"We wait until my people have him in their sights, then

you call him up."

"...I call him."

"Right. You make sure he knows who it is. Then tell him you've already located the money, that you're going to the FBI.. With everything."

"Wow, ok."

"Obviously this will be a huge shock.. He thinks.."

"He thinks I'm dead, so he panics, not knowing what's going on.. He checks his holdings and you watch where he goes.." I said.

"Something like that. Are you willing?"

"Of course. Just hand me the phone. But let me know what you want me to say, so I do it how you need it to go down." I said, somewhat clumsily.

"My dear friend, just hearing your voice will be enough. He'll soil himself."

I couldn't help a broad grin at that one.

"I'm sending a car."

"Great. See you in a bit."

With that, a steward was standing to attention with a pressed suit. It was black, the sort that all Emir's security were wearing, complete with earpiece. You had to admire him.

43

Accompanied by two other heavies, I donned my dark glasses and hurried down the stair. The air hit me like someone had opened a furnace, drawing an instant sweat on my forehead and back, but it felt good to be out in the open at last. Into the car, we were whisked away, the briefest of pauses at the gates and out onto the road. My eyes drank in all there was to see of signposts, people going about their business and buildings. Incarceration changed you, changed your perspective.

A voice came over the Bluetooth.

"Tony?"

"Emir."

"Are you ready to make the call? We'll patch you through."

"Sure, ok. Ahh.. So going to the FBI and all that."

"That's it. Nice and easy. I'll call back in a few minutes, then we put you through direct, ok?"

"A few minutes. Ok."

He disconnected and I took a couple of deep breaths. I felt awful, like my chest was constricted, a rivulet of sweat was making it's way down the valley of my back. I needed to focus. Ok. What would scare him? What could I say and how could say it? I could pretend I was speaking from beyond the grave, like I was the undead. So rubbish. I might be able to start with the heavy breathing, but the moment I'd said the first two words, I'd run out of things to say. Besides, the whole point was he was meant to recognise my voice, not hang up on a dirty phone call. I had to keep it brief though, if I was to hold my nerve. And the main point was to get him to check his accounts. Right. Then I had an idea. As I did so, the phone rang again.

"Tony?"

"Yes, Emir, I'm ready."

"Tony, I trust you. You won't let me down. Go for it."

It was the first time I'd felt an edge to him, an uncertainty.

"I'm ok. Let's do this."

"Ok."

The connection clicked a few times and I heard a digital dial. A moments pause, a long, American ringtone and then it connected.

"Yuh."

"Hello Sammie."

"Who is this?"

"Hashtag Lazarus Ten, Farzhad, who do you think it is?"

He breathed out, hard.

"Farzhad, I know everything. About Mamad and my father, about Davis. About the AyZee virus, the Swift hit, the FBI. Do you understand?"

Still he didn't speak, but he was still there.

The only thing I didn't know until today, was where you'd put the money. But I've got that too now, so... so all that remains is you and the FBI. They're very much looking forward to meeting you."

"Tony.."

"Bye, Sammie."

"Tony, Erin..."

And the connection was severed. I dropped my head in my hands. Erin what? What about Erin?

We travelled on in silence, me alone in the back of the 4x4. I looked for the drinks cabinet and after a couple of guesses located the bourbon. Perhaps ten minutes later, the phone went again.

"Well done, well done, Tony."

"You did it? You found the money?"

"He went straight to it."

"Did you hear what he said next, about Erin?"

"I'm sorry Tony. We heard only as much as you. You were perfect."

"Thankyou. So what, you can access his computer, now?"

"I'll see you shortly, we'll talk. Well done, Tony. Well done."

Thirty minutes later, we pulled into a massive, fenced spread in Santa Monica and parked up adjacent to a familiar phalanx of Rovers. I was shown through to the lounge to find Emir in front of the TV.

On it, the shot of helicopters circling and banks of police cars on the ground. The onscreen ticker-tape reading 'Breaking News: Execution on W Fifth Street, LA financial district'.

"It's too early to say exactly what happened or who the target was, but what we do know is a sniper appears to have taken two shots from a rooftop opposite the offices of Farzhad Ghassemi. We don't know if he was the target, but police, SWAT and ambulances arrived and someone was taken away by ambulance. How badly they were injured is not yet known. Eyewitnesses said the sniper fired two shots- they heard two shots and as you see, the window there is completely shattered, blown out by the impact of two high-powered rounds. Was it a terrorist attack? Again we don't know, but this afternoon, the financial district is in lockdown and the LAPD are advising no one travel in the area until they have it secured. As yet, no sign of the gunman, either. We'll keep you posted on this story and any others as they unfold..."

"Oh, it's alright, he's dead." Said Emir, switching off and turning to me for a man-sized hug, a wide grin across his delighted face. "Ah, Tony, you were fantastic, just fantastic. I was worried for a moment there, that you might not pull it off. May I be whipped for such a lack of faith. You were incredible."

I had no feeling of loss over Sammie. He'd used me as the fall guy for his plans to take over the world, had used me utterly. But it brought home how far in over my head I was and had been for quite some time. Again, an inside observer to major criminal events, even a part of it and yet, somehow still I felt innocent of any actual crime. I really needed to change the gameplay though, it was getting to be a bit of a habit. Let's hope my prints weren't on the sniper rifle, or all Hell would break loose.

"But did you get the account details?"

"Not yet. No." He looked at me once more in that pregnant way he had.

"What now, Emir? What's next?" I grinned.

"First we eat. Then we work."

One thing I really did appreciate with Emir was that he liked his food and the very best of food at that. He seemed to have life very much in the right balance of play, work and food. I mean, many people were well-off, but how many had as good a time of it as Emir? He really was a pleasure to be around.

"Have you had any thought what you wish to do when this is all over?" he said.

"Not really. More a list of the things I can't do.. I can't go home ever, I realise that.. I can't find Erin and make a go of that."

"Erin can be replaced, my friend. We all have to make sacrifices sometimes in life. This I'm afraid must be yours. But you are young, time will heal."

Kind words, but I wondered what sacrifices he'd ever had to make.

"My grandfather once said, sometimes we feel deeply, especially pain and we equate that with how much we must have been in love. But was it love, or the realisation of betrayal and the recovery from that?"

Who was his grandfather, I wondered.

"There is no rush. You must know that you are welcome as my guest for as long as you wish. I'm not trying to get rid of you, not at all, but I can't imagine you want to live on a plane all your life. Just think about it, let me know when you have a plan. I can provide you with ID, place you anywhere you want to go, an apartment in any city. You know this."

"Yes. Thank you. It's just taking me some time to adjust.. To being dead, I guess."

"Yes, of course. It would." We both laughed.

I took a shower and freshened up, putting on a the new suit that had magically appeared on the hook of my closet. If I'd ever been asked, it would of course have been a lifestyle I would have leapt at, but living it, I was constantly irked by having staff in constant attendance, 24/7. It made me uneasy, the idea that there was someone awake nearby, worrying about me and my state of being. I liked the feeling, a lifetime away now, where I was able to go home to my flat, close the door and so truly relax. Eat from the fridge, wander around in my underpants and shout at the telly. With Emir, he was presumably used to it and able to hold intimate conversations with employees present in the room, listening in. Even though I took my lead from him, I could never be completely at ease with that.

Well, whatever was happening next, it felt like we weren't too far from the end. Emir was right, I needed to think about what I did want, now I knew what I wasn't allowed, what wasn't to be. No longer did I have a car full of cash waiting for me, I was reliant on him for bog paper, never mind passport. Maybe he was setting me up for a false finish and would offload me, but I had scant options and, if I looked too closely, I might find I no longer cared.

44

For once, we went in separate vehicles up towards Topanga, so my journey was a silent one of contemplation. Looking out of the window, the orange-lit urban sprawl gave way to vegetation and wider vistas as we wound our way up off the flat valley floor, eventually to pull off the main drag and in.

Farzhad had been hit twice in the chest. Once very high on the left collarbone, but the second square in the chest. Ordinarily one would have supposed they would have preserved only the head in a case like this, but presumably, orders were orders. Emir's team had already gone someway to defrosting his cadaver by the time we arrived and Davis's familiar kit was assembled around the tank.

"How confident are you feeling?" Said Emir.

"Can you just give me a moment?"

"Take whatever time you need."

I mentally pictured the notes as much as the apparatus

around me and, with eyes half shut, I walked through the process, pausing whenever I was unsure, but I got through it all. Emir inhaled his coke in readiness for his part. I figured, if something went wrong, for the third time in my life, I wouldn't be leaving this place alive.

Emir took his position and I clamped his head. He looked up at me and smiled.

"Don't worry Tony. I have every faith." He said. I didn't study him too hard. If he wanted to lie here, then he was welcome to. Working out he had though wouldn't have helped me.

Glancing up at the gauges, the Neuro was almost at temp. I didn't want to see its face. For the fifth time, I made sure all the pieces of equipment, the needles, the wires and pipes were all ready to go, my palms sweating profusely inside latex gloves. The x-ray reminded me I already knew the right depth. Always good to check though.

"Ok, Emir. Let's do this."

I switched everything on, checking and rechecking. So long as I got the needle in with a steady hand and to the correct depth, it should all be fine. I just had to believe that and go through the motions. First the blood plasma, then the creb. I practiced inserting the long needle first on Farzhad, a towel across so I didn't have to look into his face. I felt no joy, no sense of crowing over his demise. I knew looking at him could only upset. After a good breath, I got the needle in and smoothed to the correct depth. So far, so good. I turned to Emir.

"Sorry Emir.." I put a towel over his face too and then inserted his needle. As I stood back I heard a commotion at the door. Whatever was going on there, this had to happen. I turned one tap, jamming everything on, I turned the tap.

Lastly I hit the switch, watching the millivolts register. Emir jolted, the line bolted. That had to mean success. Only then did I turn around to see what the situation was and only then did I recognise her voice. Pulling off my gloves, I raced to the door.

"What's going on? What are you doing in there? Let me in!"

I stood inside the door, wanting to go out, wanting to take hold of her, to press her face into my chest to calm her, hold her so tight, my face ensconced in her hair. But I let security stop me and I also let them stop her. They turned her around and put her back in her car, telling her she could come by in the morning. As I stood there, pressing my forehead against the cold concrete of the wall, I asked myself why I'd stopped, why I hadn't cried out to her and I knew. I hadn't faced it before, but I knew. It was because only now did I understand it was Sammie she loved, not me. Not me and probably not Mamad. It was in her voice. It was in her death, it was in that letter and it was in her face, the day she came back from the dead to see me, the day she mouthed his name through the glass, even when she knew she would never see me again. And what love it must have been, to give herself to me, only because he had wanted her to. I turned back to my first patient, gently withdrawing the towel from his face. As far as I could tell, all had gone well, his life signs were good. I turned to Sammie and pulled the towel from his. His last ten seconds had evaporated. Let him stew in this Godless place. I hoped, despite my atheism, somewhere out there my father was proud of me and could rest in peace.

45

Emir transferred to the palace and I took to my bed, with instructions to be roused if he did. It was all so exhausting. The following day I woke to the sound of birds in the trees outside and sunlight filtering through the trees and shutters. I lay there for some time, looking up at the ceiling, listening to the world outside, a brief, distant siren, but mostly birds. Reluctantly I got up, washed and went down for some food. It amazed me that I'd never bothered to learn anyone's name, not the security, on board the plane, anywhere. They were all just a mass of faceless people, there solely to serve. To be fair, I'd also been under considerable stress whenever I'd been involved with any of them and they never stuck around long enough to have a conversation. But today, I made the effort, asking the names of the maid, the chef and two of the security, though I also realised as I did so that I had no idea whether I'd met any of them before.

I wanted to go out and explore, smell the ocean, take in a cafe and look at people wandering about their business in the sunshine, but it felt rude. Besides, even if I'd been let out of the door, I would have had enough close company to spoil it all anyway, so I didn't bother, using the time to take a swim in the pool, doze in one of the hammocks and watch some trash on TV. Finally, I made my way up and took vigil in Emir's room.

As night fell, he stirred, but didn't wake directly. A full thirty minutes then passed before he opened his eyes. Through habit, I cleared the room, pulling a chair up beside his enormous bed.

"I have it. I have it all... give me a computer." He said.

I scrambled around for a few moments, before locating a Mac in his bedside drawer.

"How was it?"

"It was incredible.. Went on for so long.. So long."

With all the fuss, I hadn't watched the signals properly. Maybe, as he was such a recent death, the trip had been relatively long.

"What happened?"

"Let me do this. I must just do this..." he said, focussed purely on the screen. "Yes. Yes, yes yes. Tony, my friend, look at this." He turned the screen around and I looked down.

"What does that mean?"

"It means we're in, but we need his fingerprint and iris."

"What?"

"Standard procedure. We'll get them."

I didn't want to know.

"Right. But otherwise you feel ok? No headache..?"

"Yes I have a headache and I prefer this colostomy bag

off. But Tony. This is magnificent."

"I'll send the nurse."

Heading back to my room, my overwhelming feeling was one of stress. I couldn't wait for it all to be over. But even heading back to the plane didn't feel like an answer. What was I going to do?

It was the following morning before the medics returned from the lab with their prizes.

"Here." Emir pointed to the bottom right of the screen and I saw a number with 12 digits to it. I had no idea what it was, but understood that we'd connected. "And here.." He hit a second tab.

"There's more?"

"Two more accounts."

"Tony, you've done a great thing. Some of this is the wealth of nations."

"You can return it all?"

"I believe so. It is already known who was hit.."

"...For a finders fee?"

"Business is business, is it not? Everyone understands this. What will you do with your share?"

"My share?" I hadn't even thought of that. I wondered how much it was. I had a yen to become a superhero, travelling the globe, doing Right. Living above the law, beyond any notion of national borders, fighting crime and wrongdoing, wherever I found it. I was after all a man of Earth, not of any particular country, now I no longer existed. At the same time, I knew I'd be shit at it. I had no guile, took too many people at face value, trusted and loved where I shouldn't. However good I might feel I was, I would always be taken for all I was worth, used to someone else's own ends. Besides, all superheroes were lonely outsiders.

Even the ones who found love, it all ended badly when someone killed their chosen one.

And I realised then and there that all I had been fighting all my life, was an encroaching loneliness. Something my father had managed to assuage in finding my mother. But all my online exploration, however seedy, had been in the search for something, for someone to hold hands with, going forward.

Spinning around the globe earning and losing millions, worldwide fame- or notoriety, prison, shaking hands with and coming to terms with my own death, all of it was a lonely trail, the last of it most of all. Who could you begin to share that with?

In my total attachment to Erin, I ignored the fact that I knew she didn't actually want me. And even Emir, under all that wealth, all of that privilege, I could feel a desperately lonely man. He just had more things to paper the walls with than most.

When I took that last trip, the one I didn't think I was coming out of, it was a young man, probably not dissimilar in age to me, who had overdosed. His final journey was completely removed from his body, having vomited blood from what was presumably a haemorrhage, I felt myself asphyxiate, the drugs rendering me powerless to turn over and empty my windpipe of fluid. But then I levitated off the floor and turned over in slow motion, not in a nauseous way, but as though gravity had given up any rights it held on me and finally let go. I was floating face down in a pool. I could see my childish knees dangling beneath me as I bobbed gently in blueness. With no goggles, everything was blurred, I couldn't even make out the tiles at the bottom. But I wasn't panicked, I was just holding my breath and enjoying the sensation of being weightless, of nothingness; the sensation I had been seeking all my life, since I was that child; insulated sound, touch and vision from everything that had the potential to shock, to hurt. And now at last, I had returned to it.

'And whosoever believeth in me shall never die.'

Whatever his parents had planned for him, Nash had no wish whatsoever to stay with the anguish of living again, of that I was certain. I hadn't robbed him of anything he wanted. There was an utter sense, a sanity to mortality, this much my grandmother had told me and this much I knew.

The End

The Lake Pen Series

If you enjoyed #Lazarus10, a review on Amazon would be greatly appreciated and rest assured, there are more books coming shortly in the series...

The Big Game

Book Two in the Lake Pen Series...

What if you were offered the life of a high-roller, in exchange for laundering millions of dollars on the plush felt of Las Vegas?

Small time poker grifter Shanks is on the hunt for that one hit to take him into the big time.

A chance meeting with a shadow from his past catapults Shanks to the stakes he feels destined to play, but not without making some powerful enemies along the way.

...It'll all be worth it though, if he can just take a seat at The Big Game.

Come over to *www.andrewrajan.com* and keep abreast of what's going on. If you don't already have it, there's a free pdf gift with more information on Havasu Lake Penitentiary, plus a sneak preview from the next book in the series, The Big Game.

You can also find me on Facebook as Andrew Rajan Author.

San Fernando Press

Lightning Source UK Ltd.
Milton Keynes UK
UKOW04f0332111117
312492UK00001B/305/P

9 780993 068737